Fondly to Ellen

Tapestry
of
Hope

Alice K.
1999

Tapestry
of
Hope

Alice Kern
(Koppel Lucy)

ISBN 0-9644994-0-1

Alice Kern
6140 SW Boundary St., Apt. 201
Portland, Oregon 97221

Printed in the United States

We are a people in whom the past endures,

in whom the present is inconceivable

without moments gone by.

The Exodus lasted a moment, a moment

enduring forever

What happened once upon a time

Happens all the time....

Abraham Hershel
Recalling our Redemption

Acknowledgements

I would like to acknowledge my friends and all others who willingly supported me in the preparation of this manuscript, including Rabbi Joseph Hurwitz who read the manuscript and my cousin, Syl, who took some of the early pictures you will see in this book (he was "selected" to go to the left with my beloved Mother.)

After more than 40 years I want to thank my four beautiful daughters for being so good, patient and understanding. They always felt we were different and only now, after reading the manuscript, do they know why.

A very warm thanks to my husband, Hugo, who chose me to be his life companion from among hundreds of girls in Sweden during my stay at the convalescent home in Ahlefors. His way of living taught me how to cope to the best of my ability, to continue to live with love and understanding of all mankind.

A big thank you to all others who took time to read the manuscript and encouraged its publication. My warmest appreciation to all the Sunday School children and High School students who responded to my presentation on the Holocaust experiences by lining up to give me a hug.

Thank you all.

Alice Kern

PREFACE

For many years the time I spent in Auschwitz and Bergen-Belsen was a constant haunting horror. Yes, I did survive the Holocaust, but only because I refused to die.

In 1944, when I was taken away from my warm and secure home with Mother and two little cousins, we were told that we were going to a Labor Camp. Our lives in the ghetto, where we were concentrated away from the core of the city and its Gentile society, had become so unbearable and humiliating that when the order came to leave it seemed like a relief.

With only the clothes on our back we were driven into cattle cars. Upon our arrival in Auschwitz we were "selected" under the bright spotlight beaming down on us; Mother and the cousins went to the left. That was the last time I saw them.

All the experiences thereafter were impossible to forget, I was alive, I had my eyes open, yet my mind lived in the past. There was no future and the present was uncertain. It was hard to imagine how it would be to live again under normal circumstances — not to be afraid that your fellow citizen would hurt you, condemn you or hate you for numerous unknown reasons. To become one of the people who has the right to come and go and not be persecuted was less difficult than being able to forget the past hurts.

For many years I felt I could not function, until one day I took a pencil and started to write. Onto the pages poured memory after memory until I found myself creating this manuscript. My life until then had seemed like a pretense; I was filled with pain from many wounds, yet I could not cry or burden anyone with what troubled me. The silent, white sheet of paper took all my tears, aches, and pain. I felt reborn, finally able to concentrate on the present and even to anticipate a future. I no longer felt a need to remember the smallest details of my cherished memories. I could let them go now. It was all down in black and white forever.

The past and the pain will last forever. I had to teach myself to be human again — to love and be loved and not to hate. I did not know who my enemies were, except the few who inflicted direct pain upon me. I refused to hate a whole nation, since some good deeds had been done by them, and some had dared to stand up against the Hitler regime. A deep pain will always be inside me, yet I will not accuse one person unless I know him to be guilty.

Hatred is a sickness I did not and do not wish for. I picked myself up and started again, as I was taught at an early age. This was how my parents lived and I did not want to change the direction they pointed out for me.

Still, it seems, complete innocence is not a good thing. One should be prepared to see when others wish to inflict harm. To be alert may be to avoid the hurt. All the worldly goods left behind in the ghetto when we were taken away were lost. Nothing from my past was recovered. I could not return after the liberation because of ill health. That does not matter — I have my life.

But one memory haunts me: a promise my Mother made long ago.

I was still very young when my brother Zoli was studying in Paris to become a doctor, making Mother the proudest Mother in town. As the years went by, she kept preparing my dowry, yet the most precious needlepoint tapestry was promised to Zoli for his office when he became a doctor.

To some day recover that needlepoint tapestry, so that my brother can hang it up in his doctor's office as Mother wished, would be one wonderful reward of this writing.

The tapestry is four feet by five feet and is copied from an original painting of a French family gathered around a table covered with a white lace table cloth. An entertainer is playing for them. The father of the house is standing behind a seated mother in her French rococo dress wearing a necklace around her neck with a pendant in the shape of a T. In the original painting there was a cross, but in our religion this symbol is not acceptable, so the top of the cross was left out. On each side of the table the beautifully-dressed daughters are looking toward the mandolin player who is standing on the right side. A plumed velvet chapeau is on the carpet to his left, attracting the viewer's attention to a slight wave in the rug. It is as if the motion of throwing the chapeau down has caused the wave. Almost life-like, the small crochet squares of the table cloth are reproduced in stitchery. Then from the lefthand side one can see a part of another room with a high window with the brilliant sun rays falling through.

What a joy it would be to me to recover this tapestry. I still believe in miracles!

A picture of our family sent to Uncle Jack in America in 1930. From left to right: Heinrich Koppel (father), Elise Koppel (mother), Alice Lucy Koppel Kern (author), Oscar Koppel (brother), and Zoltan Koppel (brother). Taken in Szighet, Romania.

1

On a beautiful, sunny May 1944 morning I found myself as part of a large crowd on the street in front of our homes. We were told to stand in rows of five and wait for further orders.

I gazed silently around and the saddest picture confronted me. The people were of all ages, among them some barely able to stand up, others were small children who did not know how to stay in one place for very long, and some were young mothers holding tightly onto their babies.

One dress, one coat and one pair of shoes was all I had as I took my place in the crowd.

To one side, the house where I was born stood deserted, the windows shut, the shades pulled. It looked ghostly and forlorn. My mind feverishly searched the past with all its warm memories. Where, I wondered, were all the good times I had spent there? How could one just leave everything behind on an order? The only thing I could do was to take all the memories with me, lock them inside and cherish them forever.

We were told that the Jewish inhabitants of our home town would be taken to a work camp. For the past month we had been cooped up in the ghetto — Jewish people, herded from every part of the city of Sighet, Romania, waiting for orders. That was all that was left for us — to follow orders. This day, full with the heavy, gray clouds of war, had come upon us little by little. Not even the Hungarian invasion had shocked many people into picking up their lives and fleeing. We all, rather, developed a sheep-like mentality, shutting the ominous reality out of our minds.

Only a daring handful left everything behind and vanished — one day they just were not there. Even though the town was quite small, they managed to escape. But only a few. Most of us just sat and waited.

How much can a human take? That was soon to be seen.

Once in a while my young mind started to rebel and I entertained daring thoughts of escaping and hiding, but that was as far as it went.

How well it worked, this plan of destruction of human minds. It was not necessary to use tranquilizers. Keeping us together was enough, for we did not wish to leave our families and so stayed together to be herded off like so many cattle. It seems that the enemy always had an easier time controlling a mass of people rather than individuals. As long as we felt each other's warmth and mutual suffering, we stayed together.

Now, my two cousins stood between Mother and me. They were so young, hardly starting to open up to life. Little Joetta, seven years old, with her large brown eyes filled with fear, and Syl, her nine-year-old brother, stood there on the street like disobedient pets who had just been thrown out of their cozy homes. We all looked alike — scared, helpless, gray, sad. But on some of the faces one could still see a small flicker of hope. I would consider myself to have been among them.

This special morning, the day we dreaded, had finally come. The sun was already up at 6 a.m. when we were aroused from our warm beds to get ready for the journey.

The place became a turmoil, with people running about like ants, gathering their most precious belongings. The women were mixing bread dough to run it over to the big oven and have it baked before our journey. That was all the time we were given, as if it was all figured out almost down to the exact minute, and then out onto the streets we went.

As I stood there awaiting an unknown destiny, my gaze turned to the huge swinging gate leading to a kind of enclosed side courtyard attached to my house. On top of the gate was a semi-circular shape, inlaid with colored glass — purple, yellow and bright green. Those vivid colors are still in front of me. I remembered many, many hours of fantasizing, with their rainbow rays falling inside on a heavy wooden floor, especially when the sun shone. It was like being in a fairy tale, playing house with our dolls in this sheltered place.

After the covered porch came the yard with its egg-shaped stones laid out neatly and then the well-kept duplex. We shared our house with Mother's sister, her husband and their children. The front, larger part of the house was Mother's wedding present from Granny, since Mother was fortunate to have children soon after the first year of marriage and needed the space. Aunty Sara, Mother's sister, did not have any children until her late forties.

My fists clenched tightly from anger. It was just unbelieveable that a very short while ago this gate had sheltered me from the outside world. Why such an end to these childhood dreams?

I thought of my favorite place in the kitchen, the wood storage box near the stove. Somehow it almost helped me feel warm again, as I remembered its coziness. How I wished to be able to turn the clock back and sit there once more. On cold winter days, from this warm place, I used to watch Granny cook and Nitsa, our Romanian house helper, clean the house and once a week iron the fresh-smelling, washed linen. Once in a while I was allowed to iron a handkerchief. How proud it made me!

Everything was like a ritual: the early start to prepare our big noon meal, the light supper for evenings. Yet my only chore was to wash the cups and saucers after breakfast.

As a young girl my only obligation was to look and listen, go to school and have fun with my friends. But sometimes I wanted to do more household chores, so I would sneak behind Nitsa, down to the cellar where the water pump was, and beg her to let me pump a while, till I ran out of breath.

"Start walking!" A harsh, loud voice interrupted my thoughts. Faster! Faster!"

I glanced back after a few steps just to see how long the line was. There were hundreds of tired-looking

Jewish people of all ages, some holding onto the belongings they felt it was important to have. All those precious belongings would be cast away, one by one, along the side of the street when they became just too heavy to carry. My only blanket, a beautiful, imported silk afghan, would be among them.

Mother, her purse on her arm, carried a fresh loaf of bread she had baked that morning and still managed to hold on tightly to little Joetta and Syl, walking closely by her side. She was walking in a dignified manner as always, her drawn face betraying this pain of humiliation. How I was longing myself to be closer to her, to feel her warmth as I used to when we walked together, but I was older now and had to shelter the young ones first. One tear rolled down my cheek. Quickly I wiped it off. We had only begun our journey and the time to cry was not yet.

Aunty Sara, the mother of the two little children, had just had a hysterectomy and was recuperating in a building converted into a hospital for the Jews, another humiliation for the innocent sick ones. This left Mother responsible for Sara's two children. I comforted myself by remembering the warm and tender times she used to spend with me. I recalled our Sunday promenades, the beautiful vacations she took us children on. I felt warm and secure again.

The persecution and humiliation had started in 1940. Sighet, my birthplace, had been under the Hungarians' occupation until the First World War. The inhabitants were mostly Jews, a few Hungarian families, and a handful of Romanians, who decided to endure the suppression.

Both Romanians and Hungarians claimed this fruitful region, rich in lumber, minerals and all things that make for prosperity. To show their authority, the Hungarians required every name to end with "ovich" and the Hungarian language was dominant.

After World War I the Romanians took back the region. More Romanian families moved in and Romanian became the legal language. All inhabitants, especially the Jewish merchants and store owners, had to learn the new language. After their Hungarian schooling it was not easy for some to make such a change.

The older Jewish generation spoke Yiddish in their homes and Hungarian with neighbors. The good books and magazines were still read in Hungarian, but at school the Romanian language was taught.

Jewish life had been good, as Romanian laws were more lenient, although the church continued to spread anti-Semitism. "The Jews were responsible for the death of Jesus" was their theme, and every church-going member learned it well.

Now, the summer of 1940, Hitler had given the region back to the Hungarians. It was a quiet and unexpected takeover. The Romanians had fled and we who remained simply submitted to the new laws and regulations.

I remember the day well. Mother and I had gone to an afternoon matinee and when we came out of the movie house the streets were filled with Hungarian soldiers. There was no war, not even a fight.

The night before the takeover, my Uncle Joel heard rumors from some of his Romanian friends (officials, in fact) and was warned to destroy any past literature which might implicate him in the Communist party games he once indulged in just to pass the time. Uncle Joel was quiet and seemed rather an outcast from society, a so-called "thinker" with a mind of his own. He had a heart of gold, was helpful to others and possessed a know-how about many things. Aunt Sara worked in her established handcraft shop while Uncle Joel busied away each day without any income to show for it.

My Father and Mother worked together in their delicatessen from morning till night, while Granny ran the house and we children were either at school or at play.

Left: Granny, 1924, born in Delatin, Kolomea, Poland; married and moved to Rahova, Czechoslovakia. This picture was found in America. Right: Elise Esther Koppel, Mother.

2

We were walking now, silently. I gazed down at my sport shoes, covered with dust from the dry, dusty road (since we were not allowed to walk on the sidewalk), and I flinched, thinking of the humiliation we all were enduring, calculated seemingly by experts. Its purpose — to break down resistance and leave us as empty, worthless souls.

Then a faint smile came to my lips. I remembered how on every December 6th we children would excitedly polish our shoes for Santa Claus and put them on the windowsill where the next morning they would be filled with all sorts of goodies. The beautiful and bright red wrappings around the sweets were a sight. Sometimes a bunch of tiny twigs, wrapped with a gold string, was in my brother Oscar's shoes, to remind him of something wrong he had done. This waiting for Santa was the only non-Jewish tradition in our otherwise strict Jewish orthodox home.

The same shoes now were taking this beating and I felt very angry for my helplessness. All I could think of was that it wasn't fair!

I kept on walking, my eyes looking at every little pebble, my head not held high as previously when I was so happy and proud. My curiousity was numbed. All my life I used to walk the streets, observing every little flower in people's gardens and the houses, right and left. I knew all the houses by heart and the people inside them. I loved everything about them. I even knew every small crack in the cement sidewalk. But right now, all I felt was hatred and anger, even though it was not my nature to do so.

The houses we passed were like orphans, neglected and abandoned. We passed Csizar Bacsi's house, the small place where my favorite french pastries were baked. This was the first time I had looked up since our walk began. Till now I had been like a blind person, keeping up the ordered pace, holding back my tears. It had only been a short walk, but it had seemed forever.

Suddenly we came to a halt. We were in a part of the town where I did not often go. It was the lower part of the main street and even the sidewalks stopped. A tall, stone synagogue became our resting place. Its high, colored glass windows were glowing as the sun's rays fell on them and it made me feel good again, as if embraced by the walls of the synagogue.

One large room, with a high beamed ceiling and wooden benches, housed hundreds of tired and frightened people. According to Jewish law and rituals, women were never permitted to be in the same synagogue room with men. It must have been heartbreaking to some of the older orthodox men to see women invading their sanctuary like this. Another well-calculated scheme of humiliation.

The sun was setting. Now only a shimmer of light seeped through the high, colored windows. Was this our end? Was this heaven or hell? Maybe we were all dead, simply going through some formalities before leaving this earth?

A child's cry woke me to reality — I was still alive.

It was ironic for me to think back to the beautiful times I spent in our synagogue at the other end of town. Mother and I sat for every holiday together in the sephardic Temple, which was her choice, while Father chose a small place, more orthodox, and Granny chose another synagogue for the more elderly.

Just a short distance from our house, like everything else in our town, was the one and only temple for the modern society. This tall and majestic building, with its heavy, carved swinging door, was my favorite synagogue. It always impressed me to see the men coming and going through this door, yet the women were only allowed to use the side staircase. These stairs took them up to a semi-circular balcony framed by an artistic carved wooden railing at eye level, thus preventing a clear view of the downstairs and the men.

Up above, in the balcony, all one could hear were the beautiful chantings of the rabbi and cantor, yet I was in heaven and could not get enough of it. I especially liked the domed ceiling, painted sky blue, with the twinkling gold stars spreading a heavenly spirit.

Father's synagogue was a two-room structure with a row of windows inside which separated both room from room and men from women. In my youth, when

I was so thirsty for knowledge, I did persuade Father to take me along once in a while, even though it was strictly against the rules. How could they refuse a tiny girl who was willing to sit among all those men, looking contented and so well-behaved?

Granny's synagogue was for mostly elderly people and followed strictly the orthodox rituals. My desire for that place was not acute!

Everyone was sitting quietly, deep in their own thoughts. Since we had been told that we were going to a labor camp, some hope prevailed. We each had our survival well planned. It never crossed our minds that we might not return even though my brother Oscar, who had been detained in a labor camp in Budapest, mentioned once in a letter to Mother that some boys had been taken to Poland where they were forced to dig their own grave and then were shot into them. We neither believed nor questioned it.

I remembered when Granny used to tell me about Mother's wish to have a baby girl, now that she had two boys. This episode about my being born was my favorite story and Granny knew it. It always made me feel wanted and proud of my parents, Now, as I looked over at my mother and saw her sitting there, broken and speechless, how I wished to be able to do something drastic, anything. But like everybody else, I was helpless — sitting quietly, trying to escape the present by drifting into a happier past.

I could hear Granny's voice, softly telling me what a miracle it was that I had survived my birth.

It was late in March of 1923, during the holiday of Passover. Life in Romania then was pleasant, and all my Mother wished for was a little girl. The hustle and bustle of this holiday preparation took about one week. The everyday dishes were put away and special Passover ones, the gleaming cut glass goblets and the shiny dishes and silver, were unpacked and polished.

The most outstanding item on the holiday table, the Kiddish-cup, filled to the brim with wine for Elijah, the prophet, had its special place. The table looked like a painting itself, but for the children it was most exciting to watch this cup, for the wine would become less, signifying that Elijah was here to bring peace to the world and had taken a sip of it. Zoli, my older brother, and Oscar in his high chair watched with anticipation the miracle of this visit.

Granny was busily coming and going from the kitchen with the last minute preparation for the dinner service, while Father, propped among the huge feather pillows, was reciting the exodus of the Jews from Egypt.

Mother sat quietly beside Father and whispered, "I will feel a little upset if this will be the night for the new arrival and spoil this lovely holiday." Father glanced at her with tenderness in his big, blue eyes. "Do not think about it," he replied, then opened the prayer book and started the prayers before dinner would be served. In the middle of Father's praying, Mother got up quietly, so as not to disturb this holy atmosphere with Father and Granny deeply into their praying, went to the bedroom and asked timidly for the hebame (midwife).

The hebame arrived just in time to deliver a tiny newborn. The prayers were still being chanted around the table when she announced, "It's a girl." And then she added, "I'm afraid the baby is not in the best of health. Right now, though, nothing else possibly can be done, except to pray for her and hope." Granny left the table at this point, interrupting her prayers, and went into the bedroom to try to comfort Mother. She gently brushed a stubborn curl up from Mother's forehead, then silently returned to continue the Seder table. Everyone around the table added one special prayer for the tiny new baby girl.

A faint, thin wail woke Mother. It was the dawn of a new day and the dawning of a new life which needed sustenance.

3

The soft pitter-patter of rain on the roof of the synagogue brought me back to reality. The people, asleep or curled up on the benches, shifted as one. The rhythm of the raindrops echoed in the silence.

In the dark, slumped on a wooden bench, tired, yet not being able to sleep, I found myself wishing for a quick end.

Suddenly, lightning lit up the room. The Ten Commandments, on the top of the ark, were aglow so brilliantly that the Hebrew letters seemed to leap off the wall. A shiver went through me. Was this a sign of something or just a coincidence? No one moved; it was deathly quiet in the dark room except for the occasional sound of thunder. How I wished to be able to snuggle closer to Mother, but now we all had to be brave.

Joetta and Syl were fast asleep, leaning on Mother's shoulders. She just sat there motionless. I fell into an exhausted sleep — no dreams, no recollections, just a painful emptiness.

A piercing, commanding voice woke us up. It was dawn and we had to gather again in columns of five to continue this journey to which we had been condemned. My mind was not yet awake; my feet walked on someone's orders, and the long line of people seemed to do the same.

For a split second I felt sorry for not having used the opportunity of the night to run and hide, but I could not have left Mother behind, so here I was and I accepted it.

A few months before this journey, families had been herded from all over town to a designated area, leaving everything but the bare necessities behind. This area became the ghetto.

Luckily we got to stay in our own home, since it fell within the ghetto boundaries. Almost every room in our house was taken over by an entire family, no matter the number. Mother, my two little cousins and I occupied a room in the middle of the duplex, next to the warm kitchen, and released our beautifully furnished quarters to others.

Our salon — an elegant showcase — displayed our family treasures. Priceless antiques, lovely needlepoint tapestries and beautiful Persian rugs were my Mother's dream collection. There was a huge, solid-topped table, polished to a brilliant, mirror-like finish; a commode with doors decorated with carved apples, grapes, pears and peaches — a duster's nightmare; the 7 foot grand piano sitting next to the greatest treasure of all — the exquisite needlepoint tapestry. This magnificent needlepoint, encased inside a heavy gold-carved frame, was my Mother's promise to Zoli for his office when he became a doctor.

The salon was like a sacred place. No one was allowed or trusted to enter this room, except for when it was time for me to practice the piano, or on Sunday mornings, when Mother and I went in to dust. Now this lovely room was being desecrated by strangers — a big, fat mother with thick glasses, a short, skinny husband, and their two beautiful, bosomy daughters and a young boy. One was a school mate of mine. Pots and pans and belongings were haphazardly scattered about the room, without regard for the respect and tender loving care Mother and I gave to it. Only once did I enter the room during its "occupation," and I was so glad that Mother did not have to see that shamble.

A young Hungarian fellow came to visit the girls one day and on his way out discovered me in the kitchen by the stove and asked for an introduction. A few days later he returned with two Hungarian soldiers in flashy uniforms and shouldering bayonets. They came to take us three girls out of the ghetto to take inventory of the possessions left behind by the evacuated Jewish families.

At first I did not question the order to undertake this job, happy to be allowed to leave the dreary, depressing life. I had to ignore the enigmatic stares of the few Gentiles and policemen as we passed them on the near-deserted streets where we had once roamed so freely. But this joyful feeling of freedom was soon dissipated when we entered the vacant homes. We opened door after door, listing the precious and the mundane things that had been left behind. I became more and more depressed as I was reminded of the disrupted lives of my Jewish friends.

For several days, while I was eating my lunch during the break, the young man with whom I was working would pull up a chair beside me and begin confessing his ardent attraction to me. I disguised my anxiety with laughter, but he was persistent in his attempts to kiss me. One day, as he was bending over, I gave him a hard shove and sent him sprawling over backward — chair and all. That surprised him and cooled him off, but it also ended my brief taste of freedom.

Freedom, such a precious thing, yet I took it for granted all my life. Now I was in my twenties, free to do as I pleased, yet surrounded by a sheltered, warm home life. Even as a young child I had never had to report my actions; I could come and go as I pleased but I never thought to misuse my freedom.

I thought of Nitsa, a Romanian peasant girl who became an outcast because she had borne an illegitimate child. Nitsa was our helper and did all the heavy household chores. Her child had been left with her mother in the village and with the policeman who was the father of the child but refused to marry Nitsa.

I had such wonderful happy times with her. Hearing about her life and feelings intrigued me. She was completely illiterate, yet could make up the nicest songs and words, according to her daily moods. Many times she dictated letters to her mother. I admired the easy, poetic flow of her beautiful thoughts. Once she dictated, "As the sun in the clear blue sky, is my love burning toward you; if only the little birds could land on your windowsill and tell you how much I miss you both...." It was heart-warming and I loved her dearly.

In the cold winter mornings Nitsa would pull me to school on the sled, or on Saturday noons after school she would meet me and carry my heavy load of books as we proudly walked home side by side. Many times she carried me piggy-back to bed, crashing down among the fluffy, feather-filled pillows with happy laughter.

Only once did Nitsa dare to speak of her loneliness. My Mother sent fares for her mother and her little boy, Mihai. When the longed-for day arrived there was a handsome, 3 year-old boy in his white linen outfit, with dark hair and wide-open eyes, standing on the doorsteps. Nitsa's old and weary mother was close behind him.

The reunion was a disappointment for all of them. They just stood there, estranged from one another, not knowing what to say. The little boy, Mihai, spent the time just clinging to his grandmother.

The ordered pace propelled us closer to the main part of the city. We passed the two-story house of my friend, Olga. Oh the happy times we spent there!

On the ground floor of Olga's house, facing the street, were various businesses and above them were the spacious living quarters. There was a large kitchen with an old, built-in clay oven; then came a small room with one table, chairs and a bookshelf. This was usually as far as we got. The rest of the flat, as in all high-class homes, was a museum-like area.

The only thing I had against Olga's mother was that Olga was never allowed to accompany her friends on our flirtatious daily promenade. She had to stay and cater to her mother's chronic headaches.

Now my heart beat faster as my parents' delicatessen business came into sight. I did not dare to look at Mother, who kept on walking silently and proudly erect, Joetta and Syl seemingly her only concern. The store where my parents had spent their lives tediously working from morning till night was deserted. The gray iron shutters were closed and locked. There was no early morning bustle. This usually busy street was silent, an unnatural, ghostly feeling in the air.

As I walked I recalled Granny telling me about how Father met Mother. Silently I would sit across from her, engrossed in every word she spoke. She was a tiny woman, yet so perfectly built, with tiny feet and tiny hands, a tan complexion and hazel eyes. She was very orthodox in her upbringing, born and raised in a Polish border town, Delatine, till her Czechoslovakian husband took her away to a small village named Rahova, a village which was frequented by tourists because of its romantic setting and the underground mineral water. Granny's husband was a dentist and the only barber in Rahova until Granny learned the trade. Then all the men, even the highly orthodox ones who had never been touched by an unrelated woman, preferred her light touch.

Granny told me that my Father, who was a travelling salesman, passed through Rahova one day and saw my Mother standing in front of her house. She was a young, blossoming beauty with coal black, curly ringlets about her face as in the story of Snow White, every part of her body as if poured from a perfect mold. Father fell in love at first sight, and wasted no time. He went straight to the barber shop and asked for the "hand of their daughter in marriage." After convincing the surprised parents, who were flattered by the proposal, to accept him as their future son-in-law, he insisted the wedding should take place in his hometown in Hungary.

Granny went to her future son-in-law's hometown, Sziget, and bought a duplex there as a wedding gift. Everybody was busy preparing for the event, but no one had asked Mother if she agreed with the arrangements for the wedding or if she even agreed with her parents' choice of the bridegroom. This was according to the old Jewish customs.

Also, according to the Jewish customs, as soon as a girl was betrothed her head had to be shaved completely. Since Father was opening a delicatessen and expected Mother to help in the store it was very important that Mother agree to this ritual. Customers would not patronize their store unless Mother conformed to the tradition of the shaved head. Also, although Father was a very young man at that time, he followed the strict Jewish orthodox rituals. His mother had a wig, as did all her ancestors and all his business acquaintances' wives. Rituals were very important. Even though he could have loved Mother with her real hair, the force and pressures of the followers of orthodox religion were overwhelming and conquered all.

Mother cried for days, begging her fiance and Granny to let her keep her hair, because in her opinion to have it shaved off would be a most humiliating experience. After all, she was a modern girl, well-read and exposed to all those visitors to their village from near and far. But in the end it had to be done and like an obedient little sheep she submitted.

Finally the day came when Mother's ringlets were cut and exchanged for the wig. Granny, by providing this wig, had seemed to rebel along with her daughter. And the wig looked so much like Mother's own hair that many people never suspected it was a wig. So as soon as her own hair grew out, Mother discarded the wig and kept her happy secret. Granny made few changes in her own life which were against the ways of her parents, but she also believed in "mitzvahs" (good deeds).

One of Granny's cousins who lived in Budapest invited my Mother and her sister Sara to visit. Without concerning herself overly with the social custom against travel, Granny outfitted them and off they went. I remember how Granny's face lit up as she told me this story.

During their stay in Budapest, Granny's cousin was invited to an important ball, so she took the girls along. Mother's younger sister, Sara, was also a beauty, with warm brown hair which shone around her snow-white face, tiny red lips and huge brown eyes. People would turn to look after her.

After the two girls, in their first evening gowns, entered the ballroom and were seated, the mayor of the city sent a messenger to their table with an invitation to my Aunt Sara for the next dance. Cousin was proud to see her gliding across the dance floor in her lovely apple green, chiffon gown, and dancing with such an important person. He just had to let them know how beautiful and radiant they both were.

Aunt Sara was courted by several young, rich and handsome men, who showered her with gifts of jewelry set with precious stones or made of pure gold and silver. Often when I straightened her boudoir drawers I would find lying about such things as a ruby ring, diamond pendant or a dainty gold wrist watch. She never wore them and I was told not to ask any questions about them. Of her suitors, the man she decided to marry turned out to be controversial. Her life was not a happy one.

Uncle Joel had a jovial, happy-go-lucky personality. Extremely talented in many things, but completely impractical, he never achieved much in life; he faked a lot.

Tall and handsome, Uncle Joel spent fun-filled days flirting with maids or any girl of his choice, while Aunty Sara toiled in her handcraft business, working on her unique creations. Her wares included needle-point tapestries, lace bedspreads, curtains, and originally-designed Persian rugs. She was a natural artist, so engrossed in her creations that life passed her by without her realizing what she was missing. Uncle Joel was everywhere. His friends were the Romanian police and Hungarian neighbors. He did not want to observe the Jewish religion or, in fact, any other religion.

Once, for economy's sake, he, together with a neighbor, slaughtered a pig. He overlooked one important fact: Jewish law does not allow pork to be consumed. Although he was willing to share it with anyone who wanted some, no other Jewish person was there to share it. Once I was invited to dinner and found out afterwards that the tasty meat I liked so much was pork. People did not die from pork after all! Granny, on the other hand, was heart-broken about it and would never step into their living quarters after that.

Our kitchen was strictly kosher, with separate dishes for dairy foods and separate dishes for meat. There were separate sets of silver and even two tables in the kitchen to keep the dairy and meat products separate. This was the Jewish law, our heritage, and we all followed it faithfully.

Uncle Joel was a handy gardener and turned our yard into a beautiful, park-like place. He planted the most beautiful tree roses and had flower bed arrangements which were like those in a fairy tale garden.

He installed the first home radio in our town. This radio was small, made of black metal, and was rectangular in shape, encasing large glass tubes. One listened through earphones with small antennas attached.

I remember my first spanking, when my curiosity brought me from my bed to investigate while Uncle Joel was busy with the intricate wiring for the radio and I interfered with his work. His unexpected hard spanking sent me scurrying back to bed.

We children were allowed to listen only on Sunday afternoons to the story hours or special children's programs. Many times we had to whisk off the earphones when a painful blast of static interrupted a program.

There was one lucrative undertaking in Uncle's life. He devised the sanitary wagon for our city. Every household had a compost pile somewhere around the house, sometimes becoming a health hazard, and so he got immediate permission from City Hall to collect the garbage for a fee. The special wagon, with lids on both sides, the horses obediently pulling it, guided by Romanian peasant boys, brought a good business, until the Hungarians re-occupied the region. They did not like to see a Jew flourishing and made it a city-owned enterprise, giving a small pittance to Uncle Joel. It was a shame, just when he was finally achieving something worthwhile in his life.

Mother and I in the vegetable garden planted by Granny, 1939.

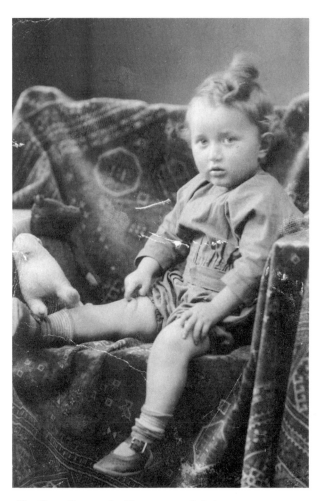

Brother Oscar, in Marmures Szighet, Romania.

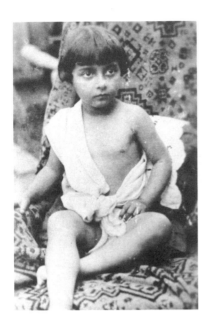

Left: Alice Lucy Koppel Kern, 1928.
Right: Cousins Sylviu and Joetta.

Aunt Sara and Uncle Joel Knacker.

Uncle Joel, Joetta and Syl, 1935. The "Vigado" moviehouse in background.

4

The march went on. My favorite candy store came into view. I had the feeling that this would be the last time I would see this familiar place and I wanted to etch it into my memory, to preserve it. The barren street corner brought back to me a sweet aroma as I remembered how an old man used to roast chestnuts in a large, black metal cauldron over a primitive brazier. The hot delicacies were scooped into our coat pockets, becoming handwarmers during the winter evening promenades.

We passed the small cosmetic shop where Mother and I shopped for beauty items, carefully choosing the right rouge, lipstick, etc. This morning, after our rude awakening in the synagogue, I did not even have time to wash my face or brush my hair or apply lipstick. I was glad there was not a mirror at hand to reflect such neglect.

My eyes darted from one side of the street to the other so as not to miss familiar stores — all places I passed so many times as a youngster on my way to school with my books strapped to my back.

A familiar street lead to the grade school where I walked every day. There was the sturdy cement double-story building, with its offices on top and jail underneath. Often we saw the men in their jail-striped uniforms sitting underneath a small daylight window, working. Always scared, we picked up speed along those windows.

And there was the grade school. For four years I attended there. Under Doamna (Madame) Filipciuc — my soul lifter, brain developer and encourager — I flourished. At the beginning of each school year Father took me to the bookstore where I got a fresh supply of paper and pencils. But at this moment what I remembered most of all was my first pure leather case, which I could either strap to my back or carry like the older students did.

My heart beat faster as the movie house came into view. How scared my fellow students and I were during the lyceum years when our teachers came to look for us at intermission. For students it was forbidden to go to see a show, yet to us it was a forbidden fruit we could not resist no matter what the consequences. Being so small, I had no trouble hiding under the chairs in the balcony to escape the searching eyes of the teachers so I was always spared. Once in a while some were caught, nevertheless our movie-going continued.

My early twenties should have been a very special period in my life — a time to blossom and grow and to enjoy the sweetness of life. Our town had been famous for beautiful girls with heavy Parisian makeup and American-style clothing. It had been very important to be up-to-date.

Then, in 1940, when the Hungarians took over, the "sky fell," bringing degradation and destruction of our lifestyle just because of our Jewish faith.

We were nearing the part of the downtown which was the second place, after home, where I spent most of my time. The business district was the hub of the city. In the center of the street was a picturesque and colorful park with well-kept flower beds which perfumed the air. A street ran on both sides which became the corso (promenade) street. The right side was for enjoying the sunny mornings while the left side was more for evening promenades. Only a handful of fashionable, decorated show windows were along this short walk, yet it was the most important way for friends to meet or to see each other, since there were no telephones. Saturdays, after he returned from the synagogue, Father would take me by the hand and off we would go. How proud I was walking alongside him, so tall and well-dressed. But most of all I felt pride when he tipped his hat as now and then we passed my teachers.

Even though the sun was not out yet on this sad morning, I looked to the right side and remembered the Sunday mornings when families would dress up in their best fineries and parade up and down. The men would tip their hats to the ladies and mutter an adult greeting and the ladies responded with the appropriate reply according to the time of day.

Children greeted each other with the informal "servus" (Hi!) but the elders demanded from them the more formal greeting of "I kiss your hand." It was very amusing for us children but I imagine it was tiresome for the men who were constantly tipping their hats to the ladies. Once in a while we all stopped and exchanged bits of gossip, then parted cordially.

The promenade ritual went on year after year until the magic age of 16, when suddenly, overnight as it seemed, we were accepted into the realm of adulthood. Our usual "servus" was now replaced with the adult greeting. As we matured and got a little bolder and more interested in the opposite sex, it was fun every evening, after dinner, to dress up and take a walk to the corso without any parental guidance.

It was my habit to walk up and down all evening with a group of giggling girls or sometimes with a boyfriend. The best fun was when the boys and girls got together and went to a very elegant sweet shop with Viennese pastries. Later, one of the boys might walk me home. Under the bright moon and with the sky filled with stars I felt so romantic, but hand-holding was the only expression of this feeling. A quick hand kiss for good-night ended the walk.

In 1940 the handsome young Hungarian cadets introduced excitement into the lives of the town girls. We each singled out one of them for a bit of flirting. Anything more than that would be forbidden to Jewish girls. Many of them in the generation before had fallen in love with the Romanian officers and some of the consequences I still remember. It was tragic when a beautiful girl, from a religious Jewish home, was found dead in the corn fields with her handsome Romanian lover. This was the solution they chose — to be together in death after their secret became known and life became unbearable.

All through our upbringing it was instilled in us that we must not stray from our faith and our people. But affairs of the heart are not easily governed by religion or heritage, especially when one is young and romantic. Each evening on the corso we would meet our singled-out cadets, but only to look as we passed one another by. It was like a ritual, just to be able to see each other even for a moment and then to happily walk home fantasizing all the way. Intoxicated, we were drawn night after night into this innocent but romantic experience.

My chosen cadet was tall and handsome with a reputation for shyness. He was about 24 years old and I was 18. I did not understand what attracted me to him in the first place. Was it his mature age and looks or was it only the uniform and the exciting thoughts entangled in my mind? Whatever attracted me, I was amused by his face, which was covered with many little freckles and I called him "turkey egg." Often my friends teased me and asked, "Well, did you see Turkey Egg today?"

One night at the theater I could not concentrate on the film. All my excited brain could do was to imagine situations including this handsome young man who was seated erectly in front of me in his immaculate uniform. Once in a while his head turned and our eyes would meet.

Finally my suffering came to an end when the exit doors were opened and everybody started to leave. All the girls I was with had to go home in different directions, so we said good-bye and I quickly turned to the left. I had lost sight of him in the crowd and dejectedly started to walk home.

It was dark, with only a few street lights on. It had never frightened me before to walk these streets, but now, how I wished he could be beside me. Then, as I approached a walk connecting one side of the street with the other, my heart almost jumped out of my ribcage. My handsome cadet was heading right toward me. I was trembling and my feet could not walk straight. Flirting and fantasizing during the promenades was one thing, but now, in real life, we were face to face and the street looked deserted. I decided that the best thing to do would be to catch my breath and behave maturely about it. After all, we were not strangers. I started to take off my right-hand glove. He gently reached for my hand and with a soft, apologetic voice asked me if he could introduce himself and walk me home. I somehow managed to reply that it was not usual for me to make acquaintances on the street, but under the circumstances it would be all right.

We both admitted that we felt as if we had known each other a long time. After all, had not our eyes met in passing many times? He walked me home with the silvery moon above us and for the first time I felt grown up. His name was Janos; he was the son of a minister.

The next day a messenger arrived to invite us girls over to the home of our friend, where one of the cadets was renting a room. There were no phones in our town so I had to gather all the guests by word of mouth. These gatherings served to help us all get better acquainted. There was nothing serious, not even a kiss, but lots of talking and flirting.

Then, at one particular party, Janos pulled me onto his lap and in front of everyone exclaimed how much he had learned to love me and that he would be willing to marry me. All eyes turned in startled silence. I sat there in shock. After I caught my breath the only thing I could think about was to joke with him, thereby covering up my anxiety by changing the subject.

Janos was angry. He sat down at a typewriter and typed the romantic words from an Hungarian gypsy song: "The one I love more than anything, a hundred times should she be cursed! That I should be her only one...."

How I wished in that instant as I read these words to throw my arms around him, and to thank him for the way he had expressed his love for me. He had made me aware of a feeling of love I had never felt before. But this taste of romance could not ever lead to anything more. Not only was he of a different faith, but the son of a reverend besides.

As we parted that afternoon I clung to the beautiful words on the tiny piece of paper and kept on dreaming of seeing him again tomorrow — only in my way — holding hands and soothing our feelings by talking. For me it was quite a revelation — I had finally blossomed into womanhood and experienced for the first time being desired by a man. We could never walk together in the daytime so, chaperoned by my friend Heidy, we used to stroll the dark side streets after dinner. It happened also that during this time a Jewish boy confessed his feelings for me. I was caught in the middle.

The turning point came in time. One afternoon I saw Janos, my cadet, with some Hungarian girls who had recently been imported to Sziget for government jobs. I felt a twinge of jealousy. This romance could bring only heartache to me, my family and his family. I was playing with fire and I knew what I must do.

After our walk one evening, Janos bent down to kiss me. I quickly said goodnight and ran into the house. I cried myself to sleep that night — I could not stop the tears. It was painful but as the days went by I discovered I was a new person — freed of a sweet but heavy burden.

These memories of my impressionable teenage years suddenly darkened as we now paced, row on row, down the corso. I glanced over to the right at our gymnasium, Liceul Domnita Ileana, where I spent so many of my growing years. The Romanians were in power then and a beautiful Romanian teacher was a great inspiration and knew how to reach us even though she was at times very strict. She displayed open affection for me and encouraged me with my dancing, helping me to overcome the fear that took all the joy out of performing.

It was the end of the fourth grade of elementary school when my teacher wrote and arranged a musical and gave me a special featured spot. We were all flowers in crepe paper tutus. There were carnations and forget-me-nots, and I was the queen of the flowers — the red rose. I was so proud, in my rose petal tutu, bright green, shiny lame body suit and pink silk ballet slippers. I was very scared, but when the time came for my grand entrance, dancing and singing, into the circle of flowers, I did it because of my teacher's support and encouragement. It was a success. A large, beautifully wrapped box of candy, sent up to the stage from my family, topped it all.

It was an entirely different story when in 1934 at 11 years of age I entered the Lyceum, a school only for girls. Somehow my interest and learning capacity just seemed to dissipate. I did not feel any personal contact and I missed the support I had had in the past. Yet I was very proud to go to school. We wore black stockings, black polished cotton uniforms, black shoes and a special beret with silver stripes, signifying the first four classes. Later the beret had gold stripes to signify the higher grades. However, I did not get to wear that one for long. The Hungarians came and everything changed, including the uniforms.

The many windows, looking out at me as if they were waving good-bye, made me recall all the exciting Romanian parades, with the grandstand for the dignitaries and the people lining the walks. The Romanian era, with King Caroll II as our ruler, was seemingly a flourishing time. The school children were indoctrinated to live and if necessary die for the King. Every morning before classes, while the flag was being raised, we stood with right arm extended and sang the hymn about the mighty king. The most beautiful melody and the dramatic middle part, which was done by a soprano soloist, gave us the shivers. But it was quite a trial to hold up our arms all during the long hymn.

Every time we would pass a portrait of the King on the street or in a shop window we had to raise our right arm in salute. All this instilled in us a strong loyalty to our sovereign and a feeling of great pride, harmony and love for the country.

At school during the Romanian era of the 1930s everyone was equal and a good feeling united us. However, outside of the school it was different because of the teachings of the church. The Roman Catholics could not forgive the Jews, the scapegoats, for the killing of Jesus. They were indoctrinated constantly, week after week, in prayer, and no wonder it could not be forgiven. Yet even that anti-Semitic teaching did not replace the national patriotism. We were friends.

The national holiday, May 10th, was an all-day celebration beginning with a parade in the morning. Grandstands lining the main street were filled with the wives of the Romanian officers and their children. It was quite a sight to see them in their colorful national costumes, their woven wraparound skirts and linen blouses beautifully embroidered with gold or silver thread.

The school girls began the parade, marching in their navy blue skirts, white blouses, white socks and white tennis shoes. My favorite sight was to see the regiment, in columns of five, saluting and marching, tall and erect in their green uniforms, followed by the most exciting parade of horses. The commanding officers on their shiny, well-behaved horses sat proudly, wearing snow-white capes, the warm wind revealing a bright red satin lining. Their plumed feather hats provided a finishing touch to this colorful picture.

I had a unique experience at one of these parades. During my preschool years I would, like a shadow, accompany my brother Oscar, to his boy scout meeting and, since I just sat there quietly, no one complained. It happened that this group was asked to march for the 10th of May parade. The leader thought it would be a good idea to have me lead the group in the parade. So there I was, on the day of the parade, a little girl dressed in a navy blue skirt, a white blouse and wearing a huge, green scout hat which completely covered my small head. With a solemn face, but gaily marching in step, I led the group of boys. When we passed in front of the risers, everyone clapped loudly and sent a shower of flowers cascading down on us in recognition of our effort.

What a beautiful and peaceful coexistence it had been.

Left: Taking Joetta for a walk, 1942. The street address during the Romanian occupation was Dr. Ilie Maris 27 and during the Hungarian occupation, Kigyo Ucca 27. Right: With my friend from Liceul Domnita Ileana, Landau Lili, in our uniforms. The closed shutters in the background indicate that it was either Saturday or Sunday.

Left: Walking in Szighet with my friends, Mende-lowich Hedy (who did not survive) and her twin sister, Irene, who lives in Israel. Right: Our family out for a Sabbath walk, 1935. Bottom: Author and Brother Oscar in School uniforms.

The "Red Rose," queen of the flowers, a choreography by my fourth grade teacher, Doamna Filipciuc, who committed suicide when our region was taken over by the Hungarians.

5

"Hurry! Hurry!" a loud piercing voice interrupted my reverie but did not disturb it. It was a past that I could dwell in and that nobody could take from me.

I could not suppress a faint smile as the police station came into view and I recalled a short but futile romance with the police chief.

It happened one evening that four of my girlfriends and I, all of us about 19 years of age and dressed up in our nicest outfits, decided to try out a new restaurant on the outskirts of the town. All of us were considered the prettiest girls of our age group. My friends, most of them dark-haired and nicely built, had developed into women, which made me feel a bit left out. I was a fragile girl, somewhat shorter than the others, but that evening I was wearing a handsome angora coat which certainly was an eye-catcher. My tiny, shapely legs still needed flesh, but my light, dancing step was always admired. This hooded angora coat helped me look a lot bigger and more mature than I really was.

Spinning angora was my hobby, which later brought me some income. I had spun the wool for the coat, then Mother had knitted the pieces and after it was dyed a specific shade, requested by Aunty Sara, the dressmaker did the rest.

So here I arrived with my friends at the restaurant in my luscious angora coat.

As we were enjoying our dinner a messenger brought a note to our table. It was for me from the chief of police. He cordially asked to be introduced later, after we finished our supper. My heart was in my throat. Suddenly I was unable to swallow the expensive food I had ordered!

I still could not comprehend a man's feelings and interest in me. One of my friends sitting at the table mentioned her acquaintance with the chief through the store where she was working. She had often delivered paper goods to his office. Rose was beautiful. Her flaming red hair was stylishly combed, she had round hazel eyes, and was quite well-developed. This was a desirable woman, in my opinion. So, I reasoned, it must be the angora coat!

After dinner, my friend Rose introduced me to the police chief, we shook hands and then all of us left.

Some days later Rose came by and asked me if I would double date with her, at the chief's request. It sounded good for my ego — I felt honored since he was probably in his early thirties. I agreed and Rose, with her date, a tall, handsome Hungarian officer, and the police chief set a date.

It was winter and even though it was evening, the brightness of the white snow turned it into day. The crisp, fresh air beat on our cheeks in the open sled sailing smoothly through the night. Only the bells on the horses' necks were audible, a happy sound to my ears.

We met in a restaurant across the Tisza River in Slatina, a town once under Czechoslovakian rule and now under Hungarian rule. The sled stopped and as we got out and entered a dimly-lit room, I wanted to turn around and run. Suddenly I realized that this was a rendezvous hideout for couples who did not wish to be seen together. For a moment I felt cheap, even though I had come with a clear conscience. But it was too late. The two men in their handsome uniforms emerged from a little secluded booth behind a colorful curtain and beckoned to us.

After we were seated, the police chief pulled the small curtain, bent over me and started to kiss me. I did not even know his name or if he knew mine, and not a word was uttered. Again, my only out was to turn giggly while flailing my arms and legs and gasping for breath — a real comic act! This brought much laughter from Rose and her escort but did not discourage the amorous attention of the chief. To my relief, the waitress knocked and entered to set the table. No sooner had she left, though, than the amorous shenanigans resumed, the chief grabbing me again and again.

I did not have much opportunity to eat, but when the dinner was over a sled pulled by two horses was waiting for us outside. All four of us squeezed into the back seat. As we approached the chief's apartment Rose asked, "Do you want to see it?" I was quick with an answer, "No!" Without any discussion I was dropped off in front of my house. A little shaken by my experience, I fell into bed, happy that Mother did not question me about the evening.

I never saw the police chief again but was glad that I had met him for one never knew when such a connection would come in handy in such turbulent times as those were.

As it turned out, I had played my cards well, because this one-time association paid off several times.

One day I was left in charge of Aunty Sara's boutique when she was taken to jail to be questioned about her husband's disappearance after he was accused of communistic involvements.

At the beginning of the Hungarian takeover, Uncle Joel was arrested and tortured by burning his toes to elicit a confession of his activities. These tactics were without result and my Uncle was released. He went into hiding and now they were harrassing my poor Aunt Sara. During the week of her confinement in jail Aunty was overcome with humiliation and bitterness. She confessed during a visit by my Mother that she was on the verge of suicide. A kind jailkeeper also warned Mother about Aunty's suicide threats. Mother must have put up bail, for soon Aunty was released. It was a nightmare for this poor, innocent, good-hearted woman. Her warm, brown hair had turned gray seemingly overnight.

It was during my Aunt's confinement that two gendarmes (police) with their turkey-plumed hats showed up at the store I was managing for my Aunt and took me to the police station for questioning.

At the first sight of those appalling feathers I turned

pale with anger. My mind and feet wanted to disobey but after the initial shock I put on a facade of bravery and indifference to disguise my fears. Stiffly and proudly I let them lead me down the street toward the police station.

We entered a small, dark room with only one small desk in it. The man in his uniform sitting behind it ordered me straight out: "Tell me where your Uncle is!" His threatening stare made me feel faint and limp and I leaned my hands on the desk for support. Angrily he ordered me to stand erect. The questioning proceeded.

I really had no knowledge about Uncle's hideaway and after a few more angry questions the policeman gave up. My heart was pounding loudly and I wished at that moment that the police chief, my acquaintance of one evening, were there. But maybe the chief was in the back somewhere because the angry voice ordered me out. I was sure that otherwise this man would have vented his fury, doing me some bodily harm.

Another incident occurred during our confinement in the ghetto that made me wonder if the chief had an influence on my destiny. Hungarian soldiers came around one morning, ordering all the occupants of our neighborhood to gather in the street. All the people from our house were assembled in the covered porch, my childhood haven.

One by one we were being taken next door into a shed to be searched. We knew by now to hide our important things, so the only explanation for this annoying harrassment was that it was just another way to humiliate us. I tried to peek through the huge keyhole. All I could see was a man's back, but I could hear a familiar voice. Yes, it was the police chief I knew, giving out orders. A shiver went through me, but also a faint hope.

It came my turn, the heavy swinging gate opened and the Hungarian soldier with bayonet over his shoulder beckoned me to follow him. I was scared, but the deep hatred inside made me walk proudly into the unknown. It seemed every time I was challenged or humiliated I grew stronger. Yet in reality I was helpless and quietly followed the soldier, my eyes searching the familiar little pebbles from our walk to the next door yard.

The house next door was situated far back from the street with a row of wooden sheds, a wooden outhouse and a well in the front yard. I had often played there and walked over with Granny to bring our challahs, cholettes, and kugels to be baked in the oven at the far end of the yard.

But now I was ordered inside of a shed, its walls covered with dust and spider webs. What was I be to inspected for?

There, in the shady and dusty shed, stood a tall, uniformed man with the hateful feather sticking out from his hat. I looked at him; I was completely at his mercy. He asked for hidden jewelry. I told him the only thing I had was an inexpensive silver necklace. He made me take it off. I handed it over to him with a proud gesture to make him feel like a robber. I felt at least that I did not lose my dignity, only a silver chain with a Star of David on it.

Finally I was told to go and my Mother was called. As we passed each other on the way my heart almost broke to see her having to go through this. I was young and could take this humiliation, but my Mother was a refined lady, proper and good-hearted.

When Mother returned she seemingly was not hurt. Some girls returned, sobbing, and related the indignities of being searched by the officer and having to reveal their private parts. So, again, I had been spared and in my mind was thankful to know the chief.

One day an old neighbor, Aunty Lola's husband, who was now an appointed official, accompanied by the feathered-hat gendarmes, entered our home and marched straight into our salon. He looked embarrassed and tried not to hurt us in any way, but they had to ask many questions about precious belongings and family jewelry. It was a frightening experience, as Mother had hastily gathered all our most important jewelry and thrown it on top of the hanging grandfather clock when the rumor spread of the house-to-house search.

How lucky we were to be saved from the ache of being robbed of our worldly accumulations. Our Persian rugs, the pendulum clock, the priceless collection of china and bric-a-brac — all were spared. But not everybody was as fortunate. I could see the horse-drawn carts passing swiftly by, filled with the confiscated possessions of our Jewish neighbors.

My feet were weary and my heart heavy as I looked down the short and narrow alleyway between the gymnasium and police station. Behind the buildings the alley widened into a park-like setting of slender-trunked, tall trees and here and there, during the warm summer evenings, there were small tables covered with white, freshly-ironed tablecloths. The gypsy music still sounded in my ears; I remembered the gypsy violinist serenading the customers and the waiters, in black tuxedos and white gloves, catering to the elite patrons. Oh, where had all those happy childhood times disappeared?

The theater was at the end of the park. Mother and Aunty Sara had season tickets for the Hungarian theater group's yearly performances. Mother's box seats on the side didn't suit me so I was allowed to go down to the orchestra pit on the main floor. The most expensive seats were the front ones. Among the other elite patrons was a good-looking Romanian officer with a monocle in his eye and an elaborately elegant uniform. He always took me on his lap to rest a while — I was about 3 years old and certainly not yet shy. I also must have added to the entertainment once in a while without realizing it, by singing and dancing along with the performers on the stage. Even today a shiver goes down my spine as I remember. It is the same feeling I used to have when the exciting moment came after we were all seated. The buzz of voices quieted as the overture began and the large, heavy red velvet curtain parted to begin the performance.

Father did not attend the theater as his orthodox upbringing denied such influence, even though he loved the music from operettas such as The Merry Widow and Lehar. How the two of us used to dance across the room on Sunday mornings! To keep my attention nothing was more soothing than music and my parents knew this.

But just like other things in life, there came the day when the theater, our one and only, was no more. It was razed and the site was transformed into a weekly market place.

We passed the sweet shop where almost daily we used to congregate. Then, there was my favorite shoe store, the dentist's office above, and the beauty shop. As young ladies we had our hair washed and set once a week and how proud I was to insist on a drop of red tint in the rinse. Many times, when seated under a light, I received compliments about this beautiful, reddish highlight in my hair.

This side of the corso had only two-story buildings standing tightly together except for an interruption now and again. One of these interruptions was a special entrance which reminded me of an earlier photograpic display. Mr. Szabo was one of the best photographers in our town and his studio was at the end of this entrance. As children, Oscar and I each won a beauty contest. We were four and five years of age. The picture of us behind the glass shelter stayed till we were almost teenagers. It must have been his favorite.

Suddenly it seemed like heavy clouds had covered the sun in our lives. The same people with whom we lived in such a peaceful coexistence all my growing years now turned against us and were not ashamed to inflict harassment and degradation upon the Jews. At any time of the day or night the Hungarian military, in their khaki uniforms, with the ugly curled-tip feather protruding from their hats, would come into Jewish homes and leave carrying away any treasures that struck their fancy.

One time, during such a daytime robbery, I lost all the lovely things my Mother was accumulating for my hope chest. Just like that, the door opened and a uniformed, feathered soldier stepped inside without being invited. He made me open the closets and, as if he knew what he would find, he ordered me into the salon and made me open a commode containing brand new textiles, lingerie and many other things for my future. My Mother was not home at the time and I thanked God for saving her from this humiliation. I was young and very angry yet I did not realize how much I had lost, since my parents had always provided for me.

We soon learned also to be careful of what we said in front of Hungarian friends or employees, as all our actions and political discussions quickly reached the ears of the authorities. When food became scarce and we had to stand in long lines to buy our rationed allotment, some Hungarians felt it was their privilege to push to the head of the line, which put any Jewish person at the end of the line again. Even the gypsies had more status than the Jews in this regard.

Only the school days for me were bright. In school one could not feel anything wrong. It happened that our school had to be trained for Red Cross duties. A grade school had been converted into a makeshift hospital to accommodate the sick Italian soldiers on their way to the Polish front. We were assigned at certain times of the day to be on hand for any assistance or to change bandages. But instead it became a song fest and fun time. The soldiers were lively and we developed quite a friendship with them. Only once did an Italian soldier have to be bandaged and the bravest among us, my cousin Olga, volunteered for the job.

Among those Italian boys was a tall, dark handsome one who told me he used to sing at the Scala in Milan. What a privilege it was to know him — Andreoli Luigi. There was also a fun-loving, fair-haired fellow from a baronial family who became extremely infatuated with my friend Rose. At times Luigi showed affection for me and mentioned how he could spend a lifetime carrying me in his hands since I was so tiny. But all this confession was over the window sill which separated us from them. Later, after the Italians moved on, I received one short postcard from Luigi telling me that he been wounded and sent home.

Cousins Joetta and Syl
dancing to my choreography.

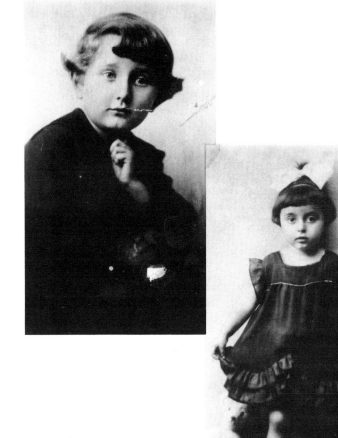

Above: Oscar, first prize contest winner photo, 1927. Right: Alice, wearing pure silk stockings sent from Uncle Joe in America; also a first prize contest winner photo, 1927.

6

The long, exhausting walk had finally come to an end — we were at the railroad station. No lingering in the waiting room or standing in line for tickets. This time there would be no comfortable train with plush compartments which in the past had transported me to happy experiences and memories. In its place was a long line of cattle cars with sliding doors and a small hole on one end. About 60 people per car were stuffed together with scarcely enough room to breathe.

When it came our turn to enter the wagon, we were barely inside when we heard the familiar voice of the Serbian soldier who had escorted the two sisters and myself during the inventory: "Stop! Enough for this wagon." He was quite infatuated with one of the sisters and many times mentioned that he was against the Hungarians' persecution of the Jews. Later we found out how thankful we should be to him, since the other wagons had at least twice as many people.

A loud, rusty squeal and the wagon's heavy sliding door closed; we slumped down on the bare floor, furnished only with a pail for our sanitary needs. I looked around in the semi-darkness and distinguished the people who had shared our house sitting all together on one side even after this turmoil, and on the other side of the wagon were a few familiar faces I knew from passing on the streets.

This began a new chapter in my life — what was to be my destiny? We sat huddled together, quiet and docile, hardly moving. But as the wheels started to turn faster and the wagons picked up speed, human nature and the animal instinct of self-preservation emerged. No longer were we subservient to the commands of the authorities. Now our rights as human beings and the need of territorial possession came into focus. People complained and fought for leg room. Children cried at one end of the wagon. However, the atmosphere at our end seemed somehow more settled. We tried to control our emotions — after all, we were all intelligent and civilized people just yesterday.

All I had to eat was a piece from the round loaf of bread Mother had baked before we left. The rest was consumed by the two hungry children, Joetta and Syl. It would be their last meal.

We didn't know what time of day it was — as if we had crossed over into a twilight zone. As I opened my eyes the next morning I prayed that this was only a bad dream, but reality hit me when I became aware of my need to relieve myself. I whispered to Mother; someone got up and passed us the pail. We went into the corner under the peep hole and Mother held a blanket in front of me. As I sat there I could gaze out of the tiny hole high above and see the sky and tops of the trees rushing by. The view reminded me to be thankful that I was still alive.

I remembered the many other trips in the train, how beautiful and exciting it was, but now it was a horrible nightmare, frightening and filled with anxiety for the future. My reputation for being the perennial optimist was diminishing. I just sat there, numb.

The second night came, and all of us young ones bunched together trying to stretch our legs and find relief from the day's sitting position. Just as I was getting settled, Lee, a boy sitting next to me, suddenly attempted to embrace me. I cringed and my first impulse was to cry out, but I did not. I shrugged him off and turned my back on him. A little later I glanced back and noticed he had managed to transfer his attention to the girl on his other side, which suited me fine.

Across from me a young lad was having trouble, among the sea of legs, finding a comfortable spot to lie down. His mother ignored his whining. I felt sorry for him and offered my leg as a pillow. I could feel sudden, disapproving anger in the air, but I just ignored it. The little boy soon fell asleep on my bent knee, but later, as I turned into a different position I discovered he had moved back to his Mother.

An arm touched me. It was pitch dark in the wagon and Lee asked me if I would like to sit up with him. He could not sleep and was lonely, and since I was awake anyway, I consented. We moved into the middle of the wagon which gave more space for the two little counsins to stretch out. The sight almost made me laugh. Lee sat on an inverted pail, with me sitting in front of him, leaning on his legs for support. He then bent down, gently took my head in his hands and started kissing me. I did not fight it this time and we just kissed on until the train came to a halt.

Once, at home, Heidy and I had invited our boyfriends, Sam and Jimmy, to her house. We sat and talked for a while, then Jimmy became amorous and tried to grab me. I turned on the giggles and laughingly slipped through his arms. He turned really angry but much to our surprise Sam exclaimed, "See, Heidy. Why can't you be like your friend? Me kissing you and you kissing me back isn't fun."

As I glanced over Jim's shoulders I saw Heidy's face turn red with embarrassment. She was barely 19 and really loved Sam, yet he, in his late twenties and with his worldly experiences, had no intention of becoming deeply involved. For Heidy it was her first love; she did not care to control her emotions.

Sam then explained to us that a man wants a woman who makes him both respect her and desire her, if it is real love. If it is only physical feelings, there is a place on the outskirts of town with beautiful hired girls for the purpose of love-making.

Heidy and I were blushing, our eyes glued to the floor. I used to watch those girls on the street and wonder about them. We also knew that they had to be under the police department's health control, but we girls never questioned it further.

The social pressure was strong. Since ours was a small town everybody knew everybody's business and saw everything. There were a few girls who got involved with lovers, sometimes Gentiles and sometimes Jews. But, of coure, they were looked down on and talked about.

One time, Aunty Sara took me to Budapest. It was the summer of 1942. Jim, my friend, was in Budapest visiting a family and the girl of the house had a birthday party. I received an invitation also. There were a few strange young men and girls and I felt a little lost and shy. But when they turned on the record player, the music made me feel relaxed and happy and I soon found myself dancing in the arms of a mediumly-built man in his late twenties. He confessed, while dancing, that it was love at first sight for him and he would like to marry me. He was a farmer, well off, and would really try to make me happy. After a few more glasses of punch he proposed marriage to me. I could not be serious at a time like this (although it probably would have changed my future) and felt secure with the presence of chaperoning mothers in the adjoining room. My giggly self surfaced once more and little by little he got the message.

During a short intermission between records we all found a place to rest and I found beside me another young man. All he whispered was, "My name is Paul." I glanced at him, smiling, and told him my name.

When the music started again Paul asked me to dance with him. He was tall and rather thin, with a dark complexion, fiery black eyes, his face broken out just like a young boy at puberty.

The dance had no sooner begun than the farmer slapped Paul's shoulder and insisted that I should be released. Unwillingly I changed partners.

At the end of the party, Jim insisted on taking me home. We walked the dark streets in silence. (This was our last walk. Since both his parents were doctors, Jim volunteered to assist the Red Cross workers. He knew first aid and it was better than carrying heavy shovels to dig ditches and railroad tracks, like most of the Jewish boys had to do. Because of his elite position Jim had enough food. Having a big heart, one day after sundown he tried to go over to his friends, the road diggers, to bring them some bread. As he sneaked away he was shot in the back and killed by an Hungarian guard.)

It was after midnight and Jim and I were standing on the street filled with people, all waiting for the street car. Suddenly I felt a slight push, and turned around to see the young man, Paul, from the party. He stared shyly at me; I smiled, then rushed with Jim into the street car.

A few weeks after I returned home, Heidy and I took our promenade on the corso on a sunny summer afternoon. We heard a heavy step behind us. By custom we usually did not look back, but somehow a feeling made me turn just a little. There, to my surprise, was Paul, the young man from the party, accompanied by an older man. My legs felt shaky and I wanted to tell Heidy who the men were who were following us, but my voice was gone.

For a split second I didn't know whether to turn back to welcome him or just to keep on walking. Since the custom was not to talk to strangers on the street, I grabbed Heidy's arm firmly and started to walk fast. They followed us until we entered my parents' store. We were both out of breath and a little shaken.

Later I found out from Jim that this fellow had

traveled all the way from Budapest with his father to propose marriage. Perhaps again, if I had turned and spoken to them my fate would have been different.

Suddenly in the predawn darkness we heard the sharp squeak of the brakes as the cattle cars came to a halt. All doors, one after the other, were pushed aside and everyone seemed to come alive.

In all the commotion a thought hit me not to look my best as I had always desired before. (As it turned out, this may have saved my life.) I put on my loose raincoat over my only dress and tied my hair in the back, trying to look older and homely.

Our door was pushed aside and a man in a gray and blue striped suit told us to step down. He even gave us a hand. Then the familiar order sounded again. "Form columns of five and hurry! Hurry!" Hundreds and hundreds of people, young and old, mothers carrying babies, all in rows were obediently moving slowly ahead. A gray-linen dressed man came closer and told a young mother who held on tightly to her baby to let an older woman carry it for her. He suggested to Mother and me that Cousin Syl should join the men's column. Apparently our silence spoke agreement for Syl left, disappearing in the ocean of people. Now there were only the three of us, Mother on my left, sheltering Joetta between us.

I was tired and sad. My arm was heavy. Mother's purse was on my arm instead of on hers. She would never have gone anywhere without it, but now it was my concern. I hung onto it for dear life.

We walked on in the darkness, coming closer to a spotlight emitting a stab of light from above. As

I looked to the right I saw Syl trying to find us and quickly I pulled him in beside his sister. Without saying much, only that he was too young to join the men, we kept walking.

Just a couple of rows ahead of us I recognized Olga and her Mother walking arm in arm and being motioned to the left. A bitter, sobbing sound behind me made me turn around. There were the two sisters from our cattle car. The older one was crying hysterically that she had a feeling that we were all going to be killed.

I looked at her, wondering at how fast a person can fall apart. She was a refined lady at home, well-groomed and intelligent, and now she appeared to have lost her mind. "Oh no!" said a man wearing a linen uniform. "Do not think such an absurd thing. No one will be killed." But he also advised all of us to be quiet and cooperative. I was willing, but not this lady. She continued to sob and cry.

A chilling apprehension went through me as we came closer to the spotlight. My feet walked, my eyes were open yet nothing made sense. The girls were going right and left as they were ordered.

The beaming lights were full upon us now. It took only moments for the German officer (whose face I recognized later on the search lists for war criminals as Mengele, the infamous Angel of Death) to motion me to the right and my Mother with my two little cousins to the left. I took a step, then rebelled and turned back as if to follow Mother, who had disappeared in the crowd already gathered on the left. Sometimes a split second seems very long; I did not even realize that a soldier with his bayonet pointing at me was forcing me back into the column marching to the right.

As I slowly walked I asked myself how come that during my childhood it was customary to walk with one's elder on the right, but that somehow in this chaos, because of the cousins in the middle, this night I was walking on Mother's right?

The bright, beaming light was replaced by the first sign of dawn, almost welcoming us to this new "theater stage setting." The line was moving slowly ahead with the woman still crying bitterly. A few hundred people were left from all those thousands we had come with. I recognized the face of my favorite girlfriend, Heidy, as she and her mother and sister walked close together. Quickly I snuggled in to their group. They were happy to take me in.

A loud, anguished cry pierced the air. The young mother had just realized that the old woman who carried her baby had been sent to the left. My eyes filled with tears, tears of pain for my own Mother. I felt very close to this stranger, a young woman crying for her baby. But what could I tell her?

Mother's black purse was still on my arm and now I clung to it more tightly. Mother had always been there when I needed her before. Now I felt forsaken.

The pain of leaving, of being separated from our loved ones, of being cruelly uprooted and torn away from our life and homes, left us numb with shock. At least in the cattle cars we were still together and in our bewilderment were praying that all this would be only a bad dream. But now were cut off from each other and from our past.

A huge cement building with bright lights loomed

in front of us. Inside were many girls in gray linen dresses. They told us to undress and place our belongings neatly on the floor. A girl approached us and asked for money and jewelry. I opened Mother's purse, to which I was still clutching tightly. For just a moment I was lost in my thoughts, remembering how as a small child I used to search in Mother's purse during the long holiday hours in the Temple, taking things out of it and replacing them.

Now all I saw were a few Pengos (Hungarian currency), a clean handkerchief and a small powder compact. The girl who looked over my shoulder scared the dreaming away. Disappointed, she left.

All our clothes were taken away and we were given gray linen, sack-like dresses. Suddenly I realized that this was how a woman prisoner looks; those men in gray and blue-striped suits must have been prisoners too. Our shoes were taken away by the girls working there and exchanged for old worn out ones. I, however, was allowed to keep my own shoes because my feet were tiny and my shoes did not fit anyone else.

The stripping continued. Our beautiful curls fell next. One by one we were shaved from top to bottom and stood there with our distinguishing identification lying on the floor around us. I stood wondering how much of this humiliation one could endure and how much more might await us?

We all now looked alike, stripped down to the bare skin and then clothed in gray sack dresses. We were a herd of young and old females with bald heads and numbed minds. We stood there till the ordering voice shouted at us to stand in columns of five, five abreast and start marching.

Our new destiny was awaiting us in the death camp at Auschwitz, May, 1944. I was 21 years old.

Top: Uncle Ily, Daughter Duci and Aunt Charlotte in Hust, Czechoslovakia. Bottom: With my poodle, Lilli. The shoes are the ones I got to keep. The curls went upon arrival.

7

Outside the sun was shining. How ironic — it should have been raining, like our hearts inside. But an inner voice told me, "Do not think, just follow orders." This was the first layer to cover my pain. The cocoon-like layers continued as time went on, thicker and thicker, layer upon layer. My beautiful life before, with its my childhood experiences were safely protected — no one could rob me of that!

The dry, hardened clay road left a cloud behind us as we walked toward the area designated as our living quarters. We passed a band of girl musicians playing in front of an entrance gate. I made believe that wherever there is music, things cannot be too bad. They were playing "Roll Out The Barrel." Although my heart was heavy, my dancing feet were eager to follow the rhythm. My brain decided against it.

We entered one of many low, clay, windowless buildings. Along the walls were bunks with a narrow walk between them. Heidy, her mother, sister, and I, along with a few girls we did not know, quickly sat on a low bunk, our feet hanging down in front of it. We were still in a daze when Heidy's mother turned to me, extremely upset, and asked, "Why do we have to be together with all these boys?" I looked at her and when I saw the disturbed look in her vacant eyes I realized that she was having a nervous breakdown. I did not answer her. She didn't even want an answer. She was the only Mother in the whole barracks. All the others went to the left during the selection — hundreds and hundreds of mothers.

A dark-haired and sturdily-built girl, manly in fact, with a heavy, ungraceful, flat-footed walk and piercing eyes, came in and strutted up and down like a general, accusing and condemning us. "All you miserable people, while you were home sleeping in your warm beds we had to work bloody hard to build this place!"

She was the blokova, the supervisor, over us — a Polish girl who had been sent to Auschwitz a few years earlier with many others to build the barracks.

"You better behave or else the crematorium will be your end," she shouted, as she pointed to a tall chimney on the horizon.

We looked at each other; we did not know why she was so furious. We were not responsible for what she had had to go through. Why did she hate us like that? Couldn't she see our bleeding hearts, our torn souls and the fresh scars of pain and humiliation?

Chimney? What does that have to do with us? All we knew as we were gathered in the street back home was that we were going to a labor camp. Killing and horror were the furthest things from our comprehension. We were never taught to hate or kill.

The blokova finally left and a heavy, fearful silence spread over the room.

After a while she came back with her work crew. First was her beautiful sister, who was like a plump, white goose with an unusually snow-white complexion that contrasted with her older sister's masculine build and rough complexion. I could not help analyzing them for a moment. Then, like something's small tail, another Polish girl followed them. She was short, stoutly built, had ugly features and seemingly was willing to follow. She also looked masculine, with a flat-footed walk.

I was wondering what they had to go through before we came that made them so bitter toward us, we who still looked like persons, even with our shaved heads. Our manners, our looks were still of a civilized human and it infuriated them that first night.

They served us a hot, terribly sweet, black water. They called it coffee. We found out later that it contained brom, a tranquilizer which stopped menstruation. The side effects were very individual — some became docile, others overly aggressive.

A piercing voice called out "Zåhl-appel!" (roll call). "Everybody out and in columns of five!" We stood there with the hot sun beating down on our bald heads. This was a torture in itself. Finally, a German woman in her clean uniform came around and counted us, while the blokova ran behind her to double check. On and on it went, 5, 10, 15.... When she passed my column I quickly took the deepest breath I could of the perfumed air she left behind; it was intoxicating.

Standing there and being counted was very important. We had no name, no age, no country. From then on each of us was only a number.

The portion of dark bread given to us brought a smile to my face. I remembered how Granny used to plead with Oscar and me to eat at each mealtime. Now, here I was eating the bread without questioning. They also gave out a piece of kvargly (very strong-smelling cheese) so old you could see tiny worms in it. I quickly gave it away. I did not like it at home and so it was easy for me to part with it. Someone gobbled it up immediately.

Then we were dismissed to return to our building and attempt to get settled on our selected coyas (cots).

Looking around, seeing many familiar faces from my hometown, gave me a warm feeling except I missed my Mother's closeness, which I tried very hard not to admit or to think about. Yet there was a haunting pain.

The blokova appeared again and as she was pacing the floor, one of the gIrls stopped her and asked, "Do you have a brother?" The furious pacing stopped and like a changed person she turned and said in a soft voice, "Why do you ask?" "Was his name David?" asked the girl, now all excited, bravely facing this pretending, but dangerous woman. "Yes!" answered the blokova.

The girl related this story.

"One day a young Polish man came to my Mother for refuge. She fed him and lodged him secretly until he had to continue his journey. During his stay he mentioned his family and two sisters and that made me think of how your face resembles the face of that young man."

The blokova listened attentively, fighting her tears, and then turned around and left. Although she did not curse us any longer or say or do anything to hurt us, we still did not trust her. But it seemed that this small incident concerning her brother made her more protective toward us. I believe this attitude may later have cost her her life.

After the morning roll call and our portion of bread and the overly-sweet hot drink, we remained outside while the small crew, who lived in separate quarters beside ours, cleaned the barracks. It was almost a pleasure to return to the barracks when they were through. It was immaculate; the clay floor smelled of disinfectant. Our coyas, with the blankets folded to one end, made it almost homey. For the moment it seemed that we could start to relax for there was nothing for us to do.

Like some daring little creatures searching for the daylight, Heidy and I decided one morning to visit Rose, whose top bunk was at the other end of the barracks. We climbed up, chatted for a while, then wound up singing and harmonizing, just like in the happy days at home. Everyone begged us not to stop. Even the blokova listened to our singing and rewarded us with a piece of bread.

Each day, as we had to stay outside under the burning sun to be counted and after that to wait for our return to the barracks, I kept searching other groups in the distance, hoping by some miracle to see my Mother. Any silhouette which resembled hers gave me a sharp pain and my heart started to pound. The search, in fact, became an obsession, even after the war was ended. (We had been told that those who went to the left were "eliminated" right away, but I refused to believe it.) To keep on hoping seemed a solace amidst the uncertainty of the circumstances and I was not going to give it up until my last breath.

As time went on and we were allowed in the afternoons to sit and visit, life seemed dangerously simple, like the calm before the storm. Being stripped of everything with nothing to do but to overcome our fresh wounds seemed a torture.

Heidy's Mother started to get concerned that after the war we girls should know how to cook. So she made our mouths water describing the intricacies of the Jewish special dishes, and with some imagination one could almost taste them. It served to take our minds off the tasteless weed gruel, mixed with sand, which we had to endure once a day. I felt fortunate that food had never interested me. At home I had had to force myself to eat three meals; in fact, I shed many tears because of being forced to finish my meals.

I remember all the insults Granny had to take from Oscar and me. We would not touch the hot fresh milk in the morning until it had been strained so that not even the smallest trace of skin was found floating on the top.

Little by little, after consuming the black, hot, sweet drink I started to become withdrawn. Any effort at conversation was a big chore and so, in my silence, I relived the past. My shrinking stomach made me dream about our busy kitchen and the wonderful aromas which would tickle our noses and the noontime dinners when my parents came home for a break. The stores closed at noon for two hours and then everybody leisurely returned till closing time. While home, Mother would disappear into the back yard to bask in the sun while Daddy and I took our naps. Later, our slow, peaceful existence became hurried and competition in business demanded longer hours. The family meals with all of us together around the table were gone, and food had to be taken in special containers to my parents. They ate in a small room in the back of the store. I watched with pleasure as they enjoyed every bite of Granny's delicious cooking. For me it was always more of a pleasure to watch others eat than to eat myself.

I remembered once when Mother decided that it was time Father should have a vacation instead of her. It was a hard job to convince him to take time off and leave his business, but one day he agreed.

Father, Granny and I piled our luggage into a horse-drawn carriage and headed for a very remote, kosher mountain resort. Granny and I were shaken up as we travelled over the rough and rocky roads, but Father just sat, looking ahead and not saying a word. He seemed deep in his thoughts and despondent over a recent apple contract venture in which his two partners had cheated him out of a fortune. He knew only one way to go and that was the honest way, so he trusted others to be honest too.

Father had been the first oil, butter and cheese importer in our small town of Sziget and sold his goods in especially clean, pink and gray, highly polished surroundings. Then as the years went by, pressures kept building. But now in this luscious, remote mountain haven he seemed relaxed. All day he walked alone in the hills. This seemed to help his nerves.

The hardship inflicted on Jewish business people after the Hungarian occupation (1940) soon became unbearable. The Hungarians were not as easy-going as the Romanians.

One warm summer day my Father, who was never sick, slumped to the floor and died. I had just come home from school and was eating my dinner when Mother came staggering in. All she could say was that Father was dead.

I dropped my fork and started to cry.

We all, Mother, Granny and even Nitsa, were crying that sunny day. In the afternoon, the body of my Father, stiff and cold, was brought home and placed on the bedroom floor which was completely cleared of furniture. Mother and I moved in with Aunt Sara for a few days. Once a day we entered the room and prayed silently. My heart was heavy, my eyes red and puffy. I remembered the happy days when we danced the polka together on this same floor, I remembered the chocolates in his pocket every Friday as we children got to explore them before he left for the services, and I remembered the Saturday walks after his return from the synagogue.

For an instant, as I watched the body, covered with the black sheet, I was almost certain he moved. I closed my eyes in fear, then excused myself from the room.

When the day came to take Father to his resting place I was furious. Almost like a wild animal, I could have easily hurt someone. This was my first death experience. The endless walk to the cemetery with the long line of relatives and friends behind us was sheer torture and humiliating. I did not care to be seen in my misery. I just wanted to be left alone. But the rituals called for this drastic walk. My eyes, red and sore, were now dry; no more tears were left in them. In a daze I just let my cousin support me and guide my steps.

Finally we arrived at our destination. As we stood around the open grave with the casket in it, the Rabbi, chanting the parting prayers, approached us with a special little knife and one by one slashed our lapels. This was like a stab in my heart. From then on I have no recollection of that day. My Father was only fifty-two years old.

Not much later, Granny passed on. I could not see how I could live without her. She was such a part of my life: her delicious cooking, the shopping excursions together, her captivating way of telling stories of the past. And she was always there when I needer her. I felt a great loss.

She was ill just a short while, this healthy, vivacious little woman. One morning I awoke to a great commotion and low whispers. I looked into the room where Granny was lying. Her mouth was foaming, her eyes without recognition, gazing into empty space. She was twisting and turning and I could see her agony. Mother quickly sent for a group of ten men, to have a minyan, and a Rabbi. No sooner had they started to pray than Granny closed her eyes and her soul went to rest in peace. She was seventy-two.

8

Right now, in this place, we never knew if there would be a tomorrow. My friends and I were young and hardly had begun to live and experience life. When I first arrived at Auschwitz Lager my happy spirit was yet untouched and I was unaware of the potential consequences of confinement. Despite weight loss, my optimistic spirit stayed on and wished badly to survive. I managed to adapt to this unknown way of life, to have hope and not to give up. Perhaps this was my salvation, to find something to cling to and wish with all my power to come through.

In a way, I was prepared to endure hardship. I had lost Father and Granny and the milk and honey days had ended some years previously. Without Granny's all-day supervision I was forced to take over the household duties for which I was so ill-prepared, while Mother was in the store with her helper, Frida. Frida also came to help me with my chores and along with Mother, helped me grow up. I loved her dearly, just like Mother did. (Jews were no longer allowed to have Gentile help, so Nitsa had to be dismissed.)

One of the hardest tasks for me was to make our beds. I used to watch Nitsa almost every day. After taking the huge feather pillows back from airing on the sunny window sills, she placed them in a special order on the bed, then covered them with a duchend (feather comforter) and all this feathery, soft and warm bedding was covered with a lovely snow-white, handmade cover with finely crocheted inlaid blocks.

Now, I had to fight all these enormous pillows and, because I was still too short to see the top of the finished product, I had to use a broomstick to make this mountain of feathers even.

I did not mind the chores, only that I felt so lonely in this huge house all alone without Granny or Nitsa. How rapid is lightning? How fast can one be hurt? Why is it that always the good things seemingly have to disappear? Is there anyone who is jealous of good times for people and has to inflict hurt as a reminder that there are also heartaches and sorrows?

The clouds quickly closed in on us, the air was heavy and the ordeals coming upon the Jews were humiliating and depressing. It was as if they were trying to kill us alive.

Our beautiful heritage was at stake when the Jewish merchants were required to keep their stores open on Saturday. What a punishment that was! For a while, my father hired a Gentile woman to guard the store. No food was to be sold. This was my Father's way of retaliation.

My little city of paradise became a living hell. Without Father, my parents' business grew less and less

— competition took care of that. Mother's goodness and trust in others was misused. I remember standing there helplessly, looking on, when our icebox, a unique piece, was taken away; we were never reimbursed for it. But times were in the favor of the strong; walking over the weak and helpless was the trend. Even Frida became involved in the black market, obtaining certain scarce items, like coffee, and completely neglecting Mother's store.

Oscar was away at a work camp in Budapest, another degradation heaped on all Jewish boys. Zoli was some place in Spain as a refugee. At least he was smart enough to run from the Germans as they neared Paris where he was studying to become a doctor.

Mother was at ease knowing that Zoli, a doctor by then, had fled on his bike over the mountains into Spain and because of his agreement to help the sick was put in a separate camp with all the other doctors. I remembered reading in Zoli's letters what a sad sight it was for him to see some of the French people fleeing, men walking and women pushing baby carriages, while he rode his bike. Everybody was anxious to be as far away from the invaders as possible. We still could not comprehend all this enmity and tried to live day by day.

It seemed in those days as if I was standing in front of a pit, with my eyes wide open, yet I could not run to save myself. We were still hoping for this bad dream to end. After all, we were decent, industrious, law-abiding citizens. Why would anyone want to degrade us, kill us?

A voice called my name. I looked across from my

coya and there was Frida, the girl from our store. Here was someone from my past and I was happy to see her. Many memories came back as I looked at her, marvelling at what a small world it was. I remembered how Mother felt compassion for her because she came from a large family; how Mother molded her through the years from an illiterate, simple girl into a refined young lady and a good business woman. How joyful we all were when the day came and she married a young tailor. But their happiness was a brief one since he was taken away to a labor camp and never returned.

For a moment I felt by the way she looked at me that she was sorry to see me here in the same predicament and all she could do for me now was to offer a small container of salt, a rarity indeed. She was accustomed to serving me and my family and displayed a protective instinct toward me. I accepted the salt, but not her pity. It was my way of staying strong to survive the storm waves breaking over my head.

This was the last time I saw Frida. She did not survive the hell. By now we were settled in our routine of life, such as it was. The hot, black, so-called coffee did its work — some girls turned to thievery to satisfy their needs, and others obtained desired items through a barter system, exchanging salt, sugar and toiletries for bread or clothing.

I sat emotionless and just observed. At times I tried to act as peacemaker among some fighting families. I was shocked and upset watching formerly loving sisters or mothers and daughters react against each other, not realizing that this miserable situation was causing them to vent their unhappiness on each other. Many times I found myself comforting younger or even older girls who were left alone like myself. This came easily to me, since I felt blessed with an instinct of understanding and was able to analyze the situation in such a way as to resolve the fights into endings as happy as circumstances allowed.

My heart was aching for my Mother, but I knew that I must bear this ache alone. I never gave up hoping and searching for a glimpse of my Mother's face among the distant groups.

One night in the pitch dark, packed together in our coyas like sardines, feet to feet, as we settled for the night's sleep, hysterical laughter filled the room and sent a frightening chill down our spines. A girl, stout in build, with a huge, round head, large black eyes, and a torn dress exposing one breast, was laughing crazily, stumbling over girls sleeping on the bare clay floor.

As the small opening threw a shimmer of light I could see to my astonishment that this was a colleague of mine from the Lyceum. She was a big girl, too big for her age. She used to have bushy black hair and two round and sad eyes. She was not popular among her classmates and I was curious as to why. She was among the top students in the class but extremely reserved and she refused to be helpful when asked a question or to do a favor. Then one afternoon after school I walked her home. After she checked inside to see if it was alright for me to come in, I entered and met her Mother. The Mother was also heavy-set and had the same large, round black eyes looking so sad, yet she greeted me with a friendly smile. After our refreshment we were sent to the drugstore to pick up some medication.

We walked silently side by side to the pharmacy where a very tall man in this thirties, with thick scars on his face, gave her the prescription. I could see her hands trembling. When we came outside she confessed that she had a crush on him. I began to understand her physical problems as well as the torturous waves of love she was battling within.

After that night in our barracks she was never her own self. It was a sad sight to see her begging for attention in her torn dress, and if we had not fought her to keep the rest of it, she would have gladly exposed herself all the way. Her irrational actions inspired the taunts and tricks of the other girls and supplied excuse for tormenting her until she broke down crying. I could not stand it and often stood up against some loud and cruel teasing. I always pictured in my mind the quiet, well-behaved student, withdrawn in her own small world that no one else could understand. Finally the situation got extreme and one day she was taken away. We never saw her again.

That incident gave our blokova an opportunity to warn us again about never letting anyone know if we were sick. We could not understand her constant irritation and warnings. Warning about what? We only saw and heard what we wanted to see and hear. Our numb minds were not functioning clearly and saw nothing wrong till one day we were forced to believe the unbelievable.

9

As long as the sun was shining and we got to see the blue sky, even though the heat was unbearable, I was contented. My hope for survival was still strong. I tried to inspire others to feel the same. Oh, how I wished this traumatic period of my life would end and that I would be able to find my brother Zoli, somewhere, somehow, and then be able to get married and raise a family of my own. These innocent wishes grew stronger and stronger each day. I wanted to live; I wanted to survive. Some other girls lost hope and did not wish for life. I told them that the only way to survive was to hope and endure. Life could turn out good or bad but the outcome always depended on the individual. Once in a while I was surprised to see an agreeing yet slightly puzzled look in the person's eyes. I quickly explained that all I could say was it worked for me and hopefully could work for someone else. I had never been exposed to studies about human nature, yet when my humanity was at stake, common sense was my guide.

In this depressing place, bare and scorched from

the hot sun, one could not even see a trace of grass or trees, only dry and heat-hardened clay all around us. Things were not any better inside. How glad I was I did not have a mirror. Perhaps the shock would have killed me on the spot! I remembered being told back home about how very fond I was of looking into the mirror and making up different kinds of acts. Uncle Joel kidded me quite often about my standing in front of the mirror endlessly, making up languages, motions, dances and songs, and how I never realized the good times Mother, Aunty Sara and Father had in the other room watching me. Aunty Sara used to encourage me to go into show business. I did have potential, only the fear of facing the audience wrecked my fun and when I just plain withdrew there was no power to convince me to do otherwise.

One afternoon, when the heat was unbearable even in the shade, we were sitting all curled up outside. I was still absorbed in my thoughts when the sound of soft music interrupted my reverie. It was the end of July (someone always kept track) and we were still being spared the hard labor others were being forced into. I got up and started to walk in the direction of the sound. As if drawn by a magnet, I disregarded the rules which said not to leave our barracks area. I heard voices around me, warning me, yet I just kept on walking. The hot sun beat down on my bald head. I stumbled over a rock and my feet were burning from the hot clay, but I just went on. After a few barracks a wide road was in front of me. Across the road I saw rows of stretcher beds with girls on them, basking in the sun. I thought to myself, "This must be a hospital and the orchestra is playing for them to make them feel better." I walked a little closer and ducked down on the side of a ditch to enjoy and absorb once more the pleasant sound of music.

The wide, open road was deserted; it was the afternoon curfew and all had to stay close to the barracks. My happy heart, pounding joyfully to hear music again, made me disregard the hazards and possible consequences. Suddenly in the distance, a silhouette appeared. I jumped up and started to run toward my barracks. It was a German soldier coming down the road.

Breathlessly I sat down close to my friends, relieved to have escaped detection. The music, my friends found out, was for the girls selected as hospital patients. But after enjoying such a luxury, the tall chimney became their last destination. Gizca, our blokova, had tried again to make us realize the gravity of our situation in this place, yet we still could not comprehend it.

In early September, the day came for us to be recruited for labor. A few Wermacht soldiers came to fetch us and the blokova could not save us any longer.

Five abreast, we started to march. The sun was still burning hot, yet it felt good to walk again. For all those months since we had come all we did was just go in and out of our barracks; the rest of the time we were sitting. I was happy to have the challenge of walking again. It was a sensation which I had almost forgotten. But my poor body, deteriorated from malnutrition and dehydration, could not cope very well. I picked up one leg after the other, on someone's order; my brain was exhausted.

We came to a gate, were counted, and then entered the streets of the town. A large sign posted above the gate read "Auschwitz." We had never heard of it before.

Only a handful of soldiers were marching beside the columns, with their bayonets on their shoulders. We all walked quietly and obediently.

The face of a curious woman appeared at a window and quickly withdrew as we came closer. The street was deserted and with no one else outside it seemed like a ghost town. But this, the perfect camouflage technique of the Germans, was our constant companion — peace but with the breath of death.

A vast green field came into sight and we were ordered to sit in the green grass and be quiet. What a pleasurable order!

The blokova, her crew and the German soldiers disappeared into the lush green bushes, leaving us alone in this paradise. I quietly ducked down to feel the cool touch of the green and tender grass, remembering all the happy times I used to spend on such grass. For a moment I felt free.

The air was intoxicatingly sweet and a peaceful silence spread over us. The only sound was the murmur of a stream below.

All of us stretched out and closed our eyes, hoping to keep this beautiful moment forever. There was nothing for us to do, so after a while some of the girls decided to take a dip in the stream. The joy, the laughter of the girls in the cool water, brought the blokova out of the bushes screaming and scolding us for doing such an absurd, daring thing — another sermon to remind us that we were not considered as humans and that we had no right to enjoy ourselves — not here, not forever.

Before sunset we were rounded up, counted, and marched back to our clay coyas. That night no one complained about anything. We just fell into a deep slumber with our lungs filled with fresh air.

A surprise roll call awoke us next day. We all had to gather outside to be counted, then a beautiful German woman, in her spotless uniform, came and selected us. Half of our group left, including my cousin and her sister, who had been told to discard her glasses and now could hardly see a step ahead of herself. Heidy, her Mother and her sister also left.

The rest of us stayed, like rejects or young puppies with their tails pulled in, lonely and frightened. I was sitting there, waiting for my fate, when an order came to get up and start walking. I belonged now among the ones who had lost weight and so could not be used for special jobs like the others who were sent to factories. But I was still alive and wanted to stay that way.

After just a few steps we entered a wooden structure and I headed straight up to the top bunk. More privacy? All I knew was I needed silence in my suffering. I curled up into a corner and tried to figure things out — my poor brain did not function well. So I closed my eyes and fell asleep.

At dawn we were called to assemble, were counted and away we went. It was a long walk on a narrow, rocky road with barbed electric wire fence on each side. At last we stopped and were told, "This is the brejinka." Here all the confiscated goods accumulated from each transport were deposited in different barracks.

We were taken inside a barracks where there were some girls' living quarters. They stayed there and they worked there. All the girls looked well-groomed, clean and well-fed. I became jealous. How I envied them. I even started to make plans of hiding among them and not following the group I came with. But as I looked at all those strange faces I knew I could not leave my few friends from my home town. We came together and it was as if we were bound together, no matter what. If by force we should be separated that would be different, but just to know that we were still together and nourished by shared reminiscences seemed to be a powerful bond.

Here, in this cabin, we heard that to our left, just a few steps away, was the crematorium. Again, I looked with my eyes, which could not see, and listened with my ears, which could not hear.

Fear of the crematorium also made me follow my group. I did not know what it was that gave me this fear, since I did not see the happenings inside of it, but I wanted to be as far away as possible. That I knew.

Later we entered a high-ceilinged, semi-lit barracks. The only thing we could see in it were bundles and bundles of clothes. Each of us was given a pair of dull scissors and were told, "Cut the clothes into strips, braid the strips, and roll the braid into balls." These balls of braided cloth were collected at the end of the day.

What a pity it was to tear up all those nice clothes. We were told the Germans used the braids for fuses. As we were busy cutting and braiding we found lots of useful things. Once we even found a whole salami inside a lining. What a treat that was! And once I found a small golden brooch with a few rubies in it. I pinned it inside my dress, but lost it later during disinfection. One girl found a good-sized diamond and pushed it down into her socks for safe keeping, but after she got a big blister from it she discarded it like an ordinary rock.

For the next few weeks we had to work night shift on the brejinka and return to sleep in our wooden barracks on the other end of A Lager (Camp A). The job itself was not hard, it was only the working into the night. I found myself staring at the scissors, my fingers refusing to move. My eyes kept on closing and it hurt terribly to keep them open. My required output of braided, rolled up balls was not sufficient. I knew it, yet there was nothing I could do about it.

One night, between working and dozing in this huge barn, the silence was broken as a girl started to sing "Ramona." It was so beautiful that the tears came to my eyes, and instead of enjoying it, I became angry, then sad, and a sharp pain went through me. Now music became like a piercing sword and I did not want to like it anymore.

Once in a while some girls left the barn and went out into the dark, into other barracks, on a searching expedition. When they returned it was clear that they had been successful. They brought back different things, including a few pairs of new shoes. As I glanced down at my feet I knew I should go also since my favorite shoes from home were now in shreds. Yet I had neither energy nor will; this infuriated the others. Once a pair of shoes were found that did not fit anyone else. They were too small, so they finally tossed them to me.

My heart was heavy as I discarded the other shoes for they were my very last possession from my former life.

At dawn each day we stopped working and went back to our barracks to sleep. Then for a while the girls went out to exchange goods among themselves. This became a booming business, but I stood back. Because of my poor weight, which was not much when I came, it was all I could muster to just make conversation once in a while.

Our meager meals consisted of bread, which looked and tasted like mud, and vegetable soup with gravel which rattled in our teeth. Once in a while we were taken to the bathhouse. We had to undress and wrap up our belongings, which consisted of one dress and one pair of shoes. These were taken to be disinfected while all the stripped bodies entered a room with many shower heads above. We each got a piece of soap and three or four girls, trying to catch the warm spray from one shower head, managed to get clean. Then we sat, naked, waiting for our clothes to come back.

Soon nakedness did not bother us any longer — we were a herd of chased and punished human beings, and our guilt was our birth. Nothing was surprising — we were there to be punished, humiliated, and to suffer, for some reason that none of us seemed to know.

Although our days looked like a peaceful routine of harmless coexistence, the clouds above our heads were getting heavier.

One night the quietness of our barracks was shaken by shouting, screaming and crying. Some of us ran to the entrance to peek in the direction of the sound. All we could see was a tall chimney, flickering and spitting sparks up into the pitchblack sky.

We found out that the sound we heard was a gypsy transport, the people crying for the last time. It still held little significance for us, even though the girls who were ransacking the other barracks were told by the Polish men that inside that building, so near to all of us, was the crematorium. Our minds could not accept that and so we just went on hoping it would not get us.

At dawn, as we were standing outside during roll call, waiting to return to our barracks, a long line of unusually tall men walked by. Their feet were bare and only overcoats covered their bodies. My instinct was to cry out and warn these men who were marching toward the building with the tall chimney. Instead, I stood there trembling from anger, not being able to help, to warn them, to fight somehow. I just stood there with the others while those men walked straight in to their death. Now I believed; there was this building with no return. The gray, endless smoke just kept on reaching for the sky and my quivering heart could hardly endure the proximity of this destruction of poor and innocent souls.

Somehow I disciplined myself to hope that my innocent wishes would come true. That flicker of hope gave me energy to go on. The will power to survive was the key. Those who did not want to survive didn't.

A loud, shouting voice broke the silence one night in the barracks as we were busily braiding: "This bundle of clothing belonged to Gizka, our first blokova!" The Polish girl told us about the many, hard-working girls she used to be with, and how after a while they were taken away and burned up in the tall chimney to become smoke, escaping for the last journey.

We just continued our cutting and braiding without a sound. We did not know what was ahead of us; we never knew. On our way back, an open truck approached with skeletons of men who were still alive. As they passed us we could see their half-exposed bodies, only skin and bone, and among them one was waving to us. How well I remembered this boy from Budapest who came every summer to visit his aunts. His light brown hair in tight curls, his round brown eyes, like a frightened doe's, were vivid in my memory. He looked so innocent and well-behaved at all times; he was polite with us girls like a gentleman should be. Now all that remained of him were those two deep, round brown eyeballs, expressing a glimmer of joy at seeing us.

After they passed we never mentioned it again.

Now, like a tightrope performer's, our lives hung in the air, but we had to wait, suffer and hope to survive!

Along the barbed wire fences some digging had to be done and one day we were taken to do it. On one side were us girls and on the other side of the fence, were the men in their gray and blue-striped linen suits. They threw the dirt to us and we had to level it. The whole effort looked senseless but we could not see the other side or what they were digging. Their faces were gray, bony and sad, almost hopeless and we were just like them.

Again we saw the results of the Germans' planning — to let us breathe, but yet not to leave, and then to make us suffer till our last breath was gone.

Among the working men could be seen the ones who were on top of the situation. It was plain again that the Polish-speaking ones were still going strong, looking like foremen, giving orders to the majority of stripe-suited men of all nationalities.

As we continued with our shoveling some of the girls from our side of the fence started to talk secretly to the men on the other side. I heard a friend of mine close by, talking to a Polish man in Yiddish, but I just kept leveling the dirt, while the burning sun beat down on us.

All I was concerned about was the little bandana I had found. I would tie it first on my legs to save them from the sun, then I would shift it to my bald head. My Mother's voice still sounded in my ears, "Do not lie in the sun for too long; keep on turning once in a while and mostly watch your head." These practical words were good advice here at the fence.

A very tall, slender man came closer and faced me across the fence. He spoke Polish, which I did not understand. Another Polish Jewish man translated it to me and it turned out to be a kind offer of some potato pancakes.

Tears mixed with a smile showed my acceptance. He then turned around and disappeared. I was trying to figure out why I was the chosen one, but when the hot aroma of the freshly-baked pancakes hit my nostrils, I gave up searching for the answer.

He handed a plate with golden pancakes and powdered sugar sprinkled on top over the wire fence, and assured me that the fence was safe right now. I took the plate and wondered what he meant about the fence.

My first bite made me feel wonderful. This was my favorite dish even at home and now, here, across the fence from the crematorium, it seemed like a miracle. The hungry eyes of my friends ended my absorption in this short but sweet gift, and I shared some bites with them. When I looked up I saw the begging dark eyes of a man looking at me from the other side. Carefully I stepped toward him and gave him one pancake. He said, "Merci!" So the French were not having an easy time of it either.

After the plate was empty I returned it to the Polish man and he smilingly took it. How I wished to be able to thank him or to say something, but this was not the place or the time, for the work had to go on.

At the end of the day, upon our return to the barracks, some girls were crying with pain, their legs burned to a crisp. How I blessed my Mother's wisdom, even though at home it had not made sense to me.

As we were starting to settle down for the night, I heard muffled sounds. I bent over the edge of my bunk to see what it was all about. My eyes caught a familiar figure. The thin, tall man who treated me this afternoon with the potato pancakes was in our barracks.

For a second my heart was in my throat. I suddenly realized that nothing is free in life. I accepted a gift and he expected payment in return. The only thing I could not understand was why me, a skin and bone little girl as it were. Of course he could not see my poor diminished body under the gray sack dress. Perhaps if his eyes could have penetrated the cloth, he would have run as fast as he could!

I knew that I would rather die from hunger than accept food in exchange for my body. Like a turtle I quickly pulled back and covered my head with the one and only blanket. I did not move all night.

In the morning the rumor got around that a man was looking for someone and since she was not found, another girl took her place. At first I felt a tiny jealousy and wanted to know who the other girl was, so they pointed her out to me. She was beautiful, with brown hair and green eyes. She came with the last transport and by then the Germans had no time to bother with the humiliating hair-depriving program. For the Germans also came harder times as winter approached.

I was satisfied for his sake that he found such a beauty. He returned in the evenings, showering her with goodies. I stayed under the blanket.

Here at this forsaken place one could act as one pleased. The blokova was not in sight from the time the lights were turned off till the time came to leave for work. For some people morals were low at home under normal circumstances, so why not here? I never condemned anyone ever, but I chose to go hungry and remain lonely.

10

One evening after our long labor at the fence, instead of being driven into our "cages," we were taken to a bathhouse. Naked, we had to walk one by one in front of a German woman and man in their immaculate uniforms.

All I had at this time was my small kerchief and the daily ration of bread and I decided under no circumstances, even against the order to turn in everything we had, to part with them. A piece of bread was more to me than any treasure. Wrapping it up as small as I could I tried to cling to it.

A selection was going on indoors and another transport was waiting outside. As we were coming closer to be selected a cry was heard behind us. It was the eldest sister of four from my home town. I had never spoken to her at home. They lived at the other end of the city and were older than I was. Many times, though, I saw these girls, elegantly dressed and with the best of manners, as they walked the corso. And especially I was impressed by a younger sister. Her face was round, like a doll's face, with round brown eyes and tiny lips, and her hair was cleanly coiffured. But most of all, I remembered her by a little satchel, with her knitting sticking out, which gave me an impression of a good and busy girl. She was tall and pretty, but always had seemed wrapped in a melancholic air as she walked, as if her thoughts were far away. I found it exciting to analyze people in this way.

Now, the younger sister who had been so pretty was selected. Her legs were swollen to double their normal size. Another girl from a prominent family in our town had to follow her. We never saw them again.

The older sister was crying bitterly, so I turned to her and told her to just hope that we would see her again, because if one is not right in the mouth of the dragon, how would one know the truth? Perhaps they would send her to a hospital.

But now, as I looked down at my skeleton body, my thin arms and legs, only bones covered with skin, I became terrified. What if they would not let me go on like this? Then, like a flash, a thought went through my mind and I asked two beautiful sisters standing behind me if they would take me in between them. They did. I did not know exactly my motive, but I knew my life at this point was in great danger. As the one sister passed the checkpoint I quickly wiggled myself after her and passed with the small kerchief behind me. Perhaps the eyes of the officer were feasting on the one ahead of me and had not time to notice me, since the other beautiful body came right after. With trembling limbs, my heart almost stopping, I was on the other side of the inspectors. Once again, I had survived a selection.

A horrifying scream made the walls almost tremble. A woman outside had run into the barbed wire fence and was burned to a crisp. She fell to the ground. The high voltage was a reality; now I believed it. She chose to end her life this way. This act of courage made us more aware of the dangers surrounding us.

No one wept for her. She was all alone and the cold and dark night swallowed up all the fear of our wondering souls.

As I was standing silently along the wall, still quivering, a voice called my name. I looked up and through a small window above my head I recognized the face. She had been a neighbor who had a store right beside ours and who had known me well. She used to admire how Mother and I dressed and our good taste. I wanted to talk to her but my smile froze around my lips and I had no words for her. She had to go and I felt a relief.

I had had a close call this night and I knew it. Upon our return to the barracks I thanked the two sisters for saving my life.

Next day our job was to carry huge rocks from one end of the lager to the other. It looked senseless except that the German woman at the checkpoint seemed amused when she could punish a girl because the rocks in her arms were not large enough.

This humiliating march, five abreast, with our arms loaded with rocks and the hot sun beating down on us, made us wish for a quick end, but it just did not seem to come. Our only release was at the end of the day, when, with our bloody arms torn from the razor-edged rocks and our feet sore from walking on sharp pebbles all day, we fell into a deep, dreamless slumber.

I do not recall ever dreaming for that whole year. This was one year in hell, a man-made hell, with no sweet dreams, only living nightmares.

To overcome all these humiliating jobs and to still survive them, I pretended all jobs were a challenge. The main thing was to do your best, to suffer if you had to, but to keep on wanting to live.

No sooner did one get used to a place than the order came to move again. Our next move was to an adjoining lager, but this time we entered a fairly good-looking building, not a barn.

Why this luxury?

There was a high ceiling, a wooden floor, even a few large windows letting the sun through, and on each coya a few blankets.

I crawled into a coya, then a few more women got in after me. We were like packed sardines, but no one cared. By now nothing mattered except to survive, and here it seemed like more of a possibility.

We were all feeling good inside this clean and bright room. Then a soft cry was heard. A young woman said, "Tonight is Kolnidre-Eve." This is the Jewish people's most sacred eve and being a rabbi's wife, she reminded us. Most of us had no conception about dates — one had to really live the Jewish religion, sincerely and strictly, in order to remember the holidays. One by one voices got together in the crying prayer, following the young woman's leading voice. As I was looking at the cool sun rays through the window I realized it was September. My favorite holiday that I used to observe together with my family was here again, except this time, in this hole, we could not indulge in human habits.

At the chorus of the crying voices, the door was flung open and the tall, blond-haired blokova came in, furiously shouting for us to be quiet. A deadly silence spread over the room. "You don't know the games these Germans play. This room was selected during the holidays a few times already, so you better behave!"

We looked at her silently and hoped it would not happen to us — whatever it was she said.

The room turned dark and no one dared to say a word. We just sat silently till one by one we dozed off, exhausted by fear.

Dawn woke us up. The window glowed from the sun and as I looked around I saw the girls, one by one, opening their eyes. We were alive and the Germans had not come last night. It seemed like a miracle.

"Zähl-appel!" called the blokova, and we all went outside to be counted. But this time I thought to myself, "I do not mind being counted — at least I know I am still alive."

A long walk was our next surprise. We knew that we were in A Lager and now we were told that we were heading toward B Lager. Here in A Lager was where we had been stripped down to skin and bone, even our names having become numbers tattooed on our arms.

The tattooing happened on a hot afternoon, September 1944. They asked for artists and after some girls volunteered for this unknown artistic job we all went outside. After passing some long tables we entered a room where the girls were waiting with the tattoo needles.

I was as scared as when I had to face a doctor at home. When the girl took my left arm and saw me turning pale, she said with a smile, "This will not hurt." Much to my surprise it did not hurt, at least physically. The pain was that from then on I was a number: Neun und siebzig-nul-drei (A-7903).

We were also assured that because we were entered in a book we would be saved and not killed. How naive we were to believe this, but anything, even a lie, was better than facing the possibility that we might be killed. One had to cling to every hope.

Soon many barracks were in sight. We had to enter one of these barracks and when it was my turn my heart started to beat faster. The semi-lit, long wooden tables on each side of the barracks were loaded with piles and piles of clothes. This brought back a recollection of another barracks — back to cutting, shredding and braiding. For a moment I felt assured. As long as we were at work we were safe.

The girls at the tables had the privilege of choosing who should stay and who should leave. Many girls ahead of me were rejected and had to leave to find a place in another barracks. As I was passing the very last table, with my eyes staring at the floor, a voice called and asked me to come to her table.

An elderly French-speaking woman gestured for me to sit beside her. I was given a pair of scissors and a bundle of dresses and coats. Silently I started to cut them into braiding strips.

Once in a while, from across the table, two good-looking French girls talked to the woman beside me. I just listened quietly and was happy I had four years of

French in school as well as private lessons. Mother had encouraged me to take French conversation lessons together with two of my friends, whose mother also believed in higher education for girls. Once a week the twins and I sat patiently facing an elderly lady with a black velvet ribbon around her neck. She spoke French fluently, but could not make us understand because her teaching capability was poor. Irene, Hedwig and I lasted one year, then we gave up, but now I was quite excited to find out that the familiar sounds were still in my ear and I could understand much of the conversation.

After the day ended we returned to our ghostly barracks. The rains had started and did not seem to want to stop. On our long walk the soles of our shoes fell apart. We arrived, drenched and shivering; there was no help; we had to endure.

When Sunday came we had the day for ourselves and some of the girls ran about exchanging, buying and selling goods. My only desire was to go to the washroom, wash myself with ice cold water, then just sit in quiet reverie.

From time to time sirens blew wildly during our curfew and no sooner had they blown than the sky was covered with a white cloud. The rumble of the airplane motors could be heard, but the airplanes could not be seen. How we used to pray for an end, even to be bombed, but they always just flew by and then the clouds disappeared. That left us, each time, disappointed and discouraged, for no one seemed to know the war situation.

It happened then, one afternoon, during a curfew

begun by the sirens, that a messenger from another lager came and secretly placed a tiny piece of paper into my palm. With a faint heart and shaking hands I held it for a while, then I started to read: "Come to the bathhouse. I want to see you. Love, Aunt Sara."

Like lightning I jumped up, disregarding curfew, and started to follow the fast-walking messenger ahead of me. Curfew or not, punishment or bombing, I did not care. My heart was extremely happy, and, most of all, Aunty Sara was calling!

I walked quickly, crouching inside as if to be invisible, with my heart pounding loudly. Then the messenger stopped and told me to approach the cement building ahead of me. She pointed out a high and small window on one end of the building, then left in a hurry. I was all alone.

The sky was covered with a white cloud, and I heard the rumble of airplanes overhead. It was still curfew. I was exposed to the two biggest dangers: being caught and being bombed. I stretched on my toes, as high as I could, and all I could see was a long line of naked girls. Suddenly an arm was waving to me and I recognized among the naked bodies, Aunty, smiling at me. She was so far away yet I felt so near now that there was a hope to meet and be together. I was no longer alone.

I was motioned to go, so I turned around and headed for my barracks. I don't know how I ever found it but when I arrived it was the end of the curfew and it was sheer luck that I was not caught on the road. It was a dangerous undertaking but it had ended well. A warm feeling went through my veins each time I thought about Aunty Sara and that rekindled hope once more.

Our daily work went on. The endless transports of people and their confiscated clothes kept on coming. We cut up the clothes, braided them, and rolled them into balls.

Each day a handsome, dark-complexioned young Greek man with a fiery look in his black eyes came and collected our work. The two French women across the table talked and laughed with him a few times during the day, although it was against the rules. I did not even dare to lift my eyes up as he went by. I always gained a satisfaction from seeing a beautiful person. As a photographer or a painter captures beauty in an artistic way, my eyes often caught such an impression. I would stare at a well-built man with a handsome face and wonder at such a beautiful creation. Often I had fantisized about being admired by one of these Adonises and now, here, behind a wooden table with piles of rags on it, a miracle happened.

It was like a bolt from the sky hitting me one day when the French women told me that the young Greek liked me and wanted me to stay after work for a while. The blood rushed straight to my face and with mixed emotion I tried very hard to cover up my embarrassment. I also wondered why he did not choose a woman who looked like one!

Somehow I regained my composure and said, definitely "No!" This was accepted with an outburst of giggles.

My heart was heavy. I felt embarrassed to even have considered the invitation, if only for a moment. Yes, my eyes saw this beauty of a man walking in and out of our barracks daily, yet I was satisfied with that only. How could such a handsome man choose me, a bald-headed skeleton like me? Was it perhaps my sad yet talkative eyes which he looked into and in which he saw my burning desire? It was plain disgusting even to think about going further than a look. More than ever I felt that survival was the most important matter, then after that were the two wishes which kept me alive — to find my brother and to find a man and have a family.

So from that day on I never lifted my hungry eyes when I heard his footsteps or when he stopped to talk with the girls on the other side of the table piled with rags. I felt like a washed-out rag myself.

At the far end of the table sat a Polish girl, rather homely, who had overheard the conversation about the Greek and myself and was willing to take my place. As soon as the day ended I was the first one to run for the roll call, while she stayed behind in the deserted barracks waiting for her lover. Just a few days passed before her wardrobe changed and she looked prettier. Even her gray complexion became radiant. Love certianly can work miracles. My miracle was in my love for Aunty Sara!

The rainy season, cold and wet, was very hard on us now. Girls came down with all sorts of sicknesses and I was among them. An infection inside my mouth became very painful and the only comfort was the little kerchief I clung to. This I wrapped under my jaw and tied on top of my head to keep my mouth warm. But the motto was, "Never complain!" One day the blokova shouted at me, "You there, take that thing off right away!" I continued to wear it secretly except for selections.

One day, as I ripped a black jacket in shreds, some green paper from inside the lining fell into my lap. I showed it to the French woman beside me and she told me it was American money. There were 3 ten dollar bills and 5 one dollar bills. How excited it made me feel. I never had seen such currency before. But that was our secret only till I returned to the barracks that night and consulted with my friends. One of them asked the opinion of the blokova and she certainly got excited about the one dollar bills. I gave her the 5 one dollar bills and she gave me extra rations of bread, sugar and honey. She also explained that once in a while a dollar bill came in very handy for paying a prisoner's way to freedom out of this hell. I knew that most of the time runaways were either killed outright or were caught and sent back to Auschwitz and its crematorium. But the escapes went on regardless of the unfortunate ones who were recaptured.

One day after work we were taken to the bathhouse and suddenly I realized that I was facing a problem: how to hide the ten dollar bills. After we had to turn in all our clothes to be disinfected a sudden idea struck me. I carefully folded the green papers very small and put them inside my mouth. Being under the shower with a mouthful of bills almost made me laugh, but I was not about to give them up though I did not even know their value. From then on, I had to go through the same procedure each time we took our baths.

One evening at the brejinka some girls found a stack of snow-white slips among the other bundles. The problem was that everything we wore had either a red stripe down the back or a circle with an Ⓛ in the middle. I asked for a black pencil and started to draw freehand a circle with an L in the middle. Immediately the whole barracks stood in line for me to draw this on the slip each had chosen. This, I thought, was my happiest night in a long time, being able to help so many girls. In my lyceum years I had wished to be a better painter or to be able to draw better, but here the determination was the magic.

To wear such a luxury as a slip was for us not allowed — one dress and one pair of shoes were all that were designated. Yet, through connections and exchanges we always managed to acquire some "luxuries."

Once, our desire for a change of dress nearly got us into big trouble. Among the piles in the barrack we discovered a whole depository of better and more colorful dresses. We attacked the pile. Now all that was needed was to paint a straight and fat red stripe from the neck down to the hem on the back of each dress. Someone found a brush and red paint and before it was time to leave the brejinka our feverish work was done.

As we were marching under the darkened sky later that afternoon, tired and exhausted, we came to a halt. Ahead of the line were German officers ordering, one by one, the girls to take their dresses off, as soldiers stood by to reinforce the orders.

Someone had informed on us!

The line of girls was long and I was toward the end, so by the time my turn came the sky was dark and the German soldier's lantern could not help the tired officers distinguish the real red stripe from the red paint we had applied.

11

Winter was close and one day, after the Germans reorganized things, Lager A was transferred to Lager B. All the girls now were in a new home and I found Aunty Sara waiting for me in Lager B. We just stood there hugging and kissing and seemed never to let go. I was so happy to have someone from my family again. We wanted to say so much and ask so much, but holding on to one another seemed to say it all for now. This was an emotion-filled reunion unlike anything I had experienced in my childhood. After our first shock and delight, Aunty told me that even though she was still bleeding from the operation she had had at home she had promised herself to survive in order to help me through this hell. She was certain that Mother had been selected only because of her children, my cousins.

Here, just like at home, Aunty Sara was my second mother. I listened to her soft voice as she tried to reassure me of our survival. It was too hard to understand what she was saying and too painful to talk about Mother. The memory of my Mother was deeply hidden and the hope of finding her was still burning inside of me. At times it was all I could think of.

Each day after work Aunty Sara and I sat side by side as if no one existed around us, silently waiting for the nightmare to end. Since our brains were not functioning as clearly as were some of the other girls' who ran about their business, we were contented just to feel close. The only sad part was in the morning when we had to part because Aunty was working in a different barracks.

When Aunty arrived she was fortunate to be assigned to help in the kitchen, which meant plenty of food to eat and for exchange. One day she brought me a most beautiful pair of sport shoes. She always knew what was best for me and this time she saved my poor feet from all the sharp pebbles I was enduring because of the worn-out soles on my old shoes. Now I felt like Cinderella — the slippers fit me perfectly.

Every day Aunty brought some raw potatoes for me; I sliced them, salted them and relished each one. She was happy to see me nourishing myself, which after a while worked wonders. One day, as we were standing naked in the bathhouse, a friend told her how good I looked, almost fat.

My work now in B Lager was again cutting, shredding and braiding — our seeming destiny. In the long and dimly-lit wooden barracks the tables were heavily loaded with bundles of clothes. I was assigned to a table at which sat seven sisters, all close in age. The older ones could not believe their eyes when they looked at me, for their youngest sister and I looked like sisters.

This youngest sister was also tiny, with dark eyes deep-set from malnutrition. Melancholy was all one could see in her eyes. I hoped my eyes disclosed a reflection of contentment and hope.

The first day we smiled at each other, just to acknowledge our similarity, then started the boring, silent job. A stout woman with a masculine build went by. She was this barrack's supervisor. Her tightly-curled, ash-colored hair was neatly combed. Her heavy, loud step gave me the shivers when she passed our table, staring at us with her steely gray eyes.

After a few days this supervisor approached our table and, standing erect, she ordered the two of us to follow her. I could see panic on the other sisters' faces, but no one said a word. We stood up in the cute little knit hats we had discovered among the clothes and silently and fearfully followed her. We had found out from the very first day at Auschwitz that any particular fear did not last for long — one frightening happening always followed another. Our short walk on the deserted road felt almost exciting.

The blokova stopped in front of a large barn with tall and narrow swinging doors. She opened one side, entered quietly, and motioned to us to follow her. The two of us did not know the reason for this excursion, but this was not the time or place to question the blokova, so we entered. At first we stood close to the door to be able to run in case of danger, but after we looked around and saw no danger we stepped in cautiously. We were not sure what kind of danger our senses had been alerted for.

Actually this barn looked like a gold mine to us.

There were huge piles of clothes thrown all around and we did not even realize that the blokova had disappeared. Choosing the thin, easy-to-cut pieces we kept so busy that it was a shock to the two of us when we realized that a young man was watching us in silence. He stood at a distance, smiling. We got so frightened that, almost stepping on each other, we stood very close together and murmured as if we were searching for something on the floor, pretending that we did not see him.

He then said something in Polish. We took a very deep breath and continued to tie a bundle to take back to the barracks. Since he received no answer, he turned around and left. Perhaps we missed an opportunity with this young Polish man, but that was our choice.

After some time the supervisor came out from a door behind all the piles of clothes and told us to start walking back. The sisters let out a sigh of relief to see us again. From that day on the supervisor never came again, but our little excursion, looking back on it, made us somehow proud to have been the chosen ones.

The early winter dawn froze our bones stiff as we stood for roll call. Not even the still, bright stars way up high could help us. The only thing left was to stand closer to one another for body heat.

Seemingly the war for the Germans had come to a turning point. One day some nurses came to collect blood from us. Some of the girls volunteered in exchange for some bread and liverwurst, but I hid each time they came around. My diminished weight left me only skin and bone with only the willpower to live keeping me alive.

The time came again for our bath. We had come to dread this by now, since one never knew if one would be alive after it or be selected and sent up in smoke.

Outside in the waiting line a well-dressed Polish girl was squabbling with an elderly, Greek-speaking woman with two daughters. The younger daughter was clinging to the woman and the other, older daughter tried to defend her mother. The Polish girl started to speak Yiddish to me and on the other side the Greek girl spoke French to me. I found myself translating for the two parties and also trying to make them understand that the clothes this elderly Greek woman had snatched were for her young child and how the Polish girl just had to forgive them since she had the best outfit on anyway.

The squabble stopped and the older sister introduced herself and thanked me over and over for the happy ending. I took my place in line again just in time to start our walk into the bathhouse.

Inside, the huge room was empty. There were windows and a cold cement floor. Our clothes were taken to be disinfected, then came the shower. Afterwards we were sitting, naked and shivering, waiting for our dresses, when my thoughts turned to how I would survive a winter without a coat. No one had seemed to care about our wardrobe and winter was here.

Suddenly a jacket landed at my feet. A Greek man was throwing them around and I grabbed one. It was like a prayer had been answered.

The Greek girl came to me and whispered that she knew some of the boys working in the back and had asked them to be sure to throw one for me. I was very grateful. As she was leaving she said, "My name is Lisetta, and thank you again!"

At the barracks I saw all the girls standing outside. It was another move or another selection. I hurried to find Aunty Sara. I snuggled close to her and, like two people and one soul, we prepared for anything to come. The Germans never failed in surprises.

It was the end of a hard day's work, the sky was dark and we had not had our evening meal, but we had to go to another barracks, a partially-lit wooden barracks with the three-layered wooden coyas on each side. The room was quickly filled to capacity with cold and hungry women, fighting for a small corner to rest in.

I asked Aunty if she would mind climbing up with me and looking for a top bunk. As we were stepping carefully over some girls' legs one of them stopped me and asked, "Aren't you the one who came once to Hust wearing an angora coat?"

I could not see her face in the dark corner and I was glad she could not see my blushing as I quickly nodded and passed her. I sat down beside Aunty Sara and trembled as I remembered my unique coat, the one and only angora coat in our whole town and many others. But right now, to think was painful.

I had just pulled a blanket over me and stretched out when a girl called up to us: "The blokova wants to see you." Tired and hungry, I went to face the blokova. She turned out to be a girl who had worked in the bakery next to our store at home. She muttered that my Mother had been very kind to her and offered me a piping hot bowl of soup. I ate it, excused myself and left.

This had been an emotional evening for me, a tearing open of my wounds, but I was also very grateful for it.

The one small light was turned off, our weary souls turned to rest. Suddenly, cracks, crashes and a horrifying screaming filled the pitch dark barn.

Across from us a three-layer bunk had collapsed and crushed people on the lowest bunk to death. We did not dare to move much in our coyas. The dead bodies were taken out on a stretcher and, as if nothing had happened, we all fell asleep. Our human instinct by now was trained not to react, but only to carry on and try to survive.

Next morning no one mentioned the tragedy. We had our hot, black water and a ration of the daily bread and then off we went to work.

Our ability to feel was being lost. Being driven to and fro like cattle we had no chance to think. We became numbed even to the unfairness of the well-dressed German woman, all bundled up in her winter coat, while we were waiting, freezing, outside in the cold to be counted each star-lit dawn.

Once again, only this time in the middle of the afternoon while we were at our labor, the order came to stand up and start walking toward the bathhouse. The frosty road was crackling under our feet and a terrifying feeling haunted us; one never knew if there would be a return, but I tried to convince myself as I always used to do: "Wait and see."

We entered the bone-chilling cement building

where hundreds and hundreds of girls were slowly moving forward. No one could see what was ahead, so I started to look for familiar faces. Without Aunty Sara I felt doomed.

Among all those bald heads I did find one person I knew — Cousin Irene. I approached her and she told me that her group was leaving to work somewhere in Germany. I told her about my good fortune of finding the bills and she suggested that I should hide them inside my bread. Carefully I dug out a piece of the bread and folding the bills as small as possible, I placed them in the small cavity, then pressed the piece back tightly. My small kerchief looked harmless, but my secret treasure was inside.

Our clothes were taken and the selection was done; a few of us had to remain behind. Stark naked, skin and bone, I suddenly realized that this was the end. The others passed the selection but we had not. Immediately my mind started to work feverishly. Just in case we would be taken to the crematorium, could I offer the money in exchange for my life? I shrank at the thought, but it was an option. No more rumors — this was it.

A tall, very slender man with a clean-shaven head, protruding cheekbones and deep-set, cold, glassy eyes, walked in. He walked by us, twenty some girls, standing stark naked. As this Polish-speaking man passed, one could feel the cold breeze of Death; he was sent to take us to the crematorium.

I did not cry. I must have been completely frozen. I had no fear, no tears, only a passion somehow to be able to save my life.

We had heard about other occasions like this, but until one experiences it oneself it is impossible to believe it. My concern at the moment was to stand behind the front row, to hide my naked body, which I had never revealed so obviously in front of a man. Even as a child I was very conscious of nakedness and when we girlfriends had to change clothes, I was always far in a corner. How I wished now that the earth would open, but the ghostly-looking man did not seem to really see us. All he was concerned with was to count us so we could be appropriately handled upon arrival.

Then, as he was starting to leave, a girl burst out in an hysterical cry. "This is a Capo (crematorium supervisor); he will take us to the crematorium!" I looked at the girl next to me, perhaps wanting to hear a contradiction, but knowing that the crying girl was right. I froze. I was face to face with death yet still hoping somehow to escape.

The pleading apparently touched him. He turned around and left the room. Now with a slight flicker of hope, we stood there waiting, chilled to the bone. The door was flung open and a very good-looking, tall officer came in with the Capo behind him. Proudly and briskly he marched up and down in front of us. The Capo, who addressed the officer as Mengele, was at this point also pleading with him, but Mengele disappeared and the Capo stood there seemingly disappointed.

He asked us to go into another room, holding the door open for us. The girls were crying but one by one we entered. It was a room with toilets, a bare, cold cement floor and a tiny window way up high letting the late rays of the sun through.

Exhausted, I leaned against the cold cement wall, not feeling the shivers it caused, and kept on thinking how to buy my life when the right moment would come. My eyes were dry — everything within me had dried up long ago. The rumor was now a reality: the flaming chimneys in the dark; the screams of the Gypsies, and tall naked men with only their overcoats covering their naked bodies, marching, as we had never dared to admit, straight into the crematorium; the prominent attorney from our home town finding his own father among the cadavers as he pulled gold teeth as his job for the Lager; the gas showerheads.

Yes, now I believed all these things. I had no choice and I came to accept my destiny, hoping it would be painless.

12

The door opened and a girl with a friendly voice told us to leave this place and follow her into another room. Very slowly and careful of every step we took, we entered an empty square room with bright lights and a few windows around the walls.

Seeing windows somehow brought me peace of mind, but first we had to make sure that there were no shower heads above us. It had happened on a previous occasion that when we were taken to have our bath one of the girls discovered the different shape of the shower heads. How unusual it seemed to me to make a fuss about a shower head. From then on, though, each time we had to take a shower, we were careful to first check the shower heads.

We looked up, looked down, then finally we started to breathe again. No, there was nothing threatening looking; the room was warm and bright.

Although still shivering from the other place and waiting for our death call, we started to loosen up and the blood in our frozen veins began to flow again. Ironically, all this heat and light seemed to welcome us back to life after a close call with death.

It must have been hours we waited, outside it was dark. We had no idea why, but suddenly the lights went out and all turned dark inside as well. The loud sirens outside made us tremble with joy. We could hear the airplanes right above us. Oh how we prayed for the bombs to fall!

But nothing happened, the sounds stopped, the noise died down, and all of us, disappointed but still alive, sat there till the lights came on again. The door opened and the familiar face of our blokova appeared. Our clothes were returned and she ordered us to dress quickly and follow her.

Still in a daze after this torturous afternnon, walking on the frozen road back to our barracks, we could not believe our reprieve. Then I recalled hearing once that if the Germans heard that the selected group found out about their destiny, they did not execute the death sentence. Whether that was true or not, I didn't know — only that it had seemingly worked for us.

It was past midnight when we returned, only to find that everybody had been shifted around. Sheer luck helped me to find Aunty Sara who was sitting and waiting for me.

My cousin, who was returned to the barracks instead of being sent to work, told me the next day that Aunty Sara had cried all evening and prayed, not even touching her meager supper.

That night I fell asleep in Aunty Sara's arms and when I awakened her arms were still around me. After that she never left me. She offered the blokova to knit her some warm underwear in return for being able to keep me with her by her side. So each day we went into the quarters of the Polish blokova and knitted underwear for her till the end of the day, when we had to return to our barracks.

For the two of us it was only a few short, sheltered days till the order came to evacuate Auschwitz. The enemy was closing in.

It was early morning, a cold but sunny morning, as we were standing outside waiting for marching orders, that we each got two loaves of bread. They were very dark and very heavy and it crossed my mind to just leave them behind but this was a treasure like never before. The only thing was that instead of being able to eat it, we had to start walking. What a contradiction — our undernourished bodies and the two loaves under our arms. Perhaps it was all figured out in case we should be captured, to show the world the plenty we had here.

There were only a handful of young boys in German uniforms on each side of the columns of hundreds of girls as we started to move. As they say, it takes one good sheep dog to chase a huge herd into a corral. This was the case with us.

We felt a relief in leaving this hell behind us: the smoking crematorium which we had missed by sheer luck and the stringent labor inflicted upon us. What worse could there be?

The glittering snow on the road was almost blinding under the sun. Such a beautiful sight, just like on a winter morning back home. Our destiny was ahead of us and we were ready.

The first steps were painful after having sat all day, every day, for so many months, but after a while our feet picked up the rhythm. We had to walk, it was an order, and order was the magic word. Young and old alike, we were driven toward our new destination and there was no time or thought to ask questions or oppose orders. Only later did we find out that a few sick girls had hid in Auschwitz and were liberated the following day by the Russian army and the Allies.

Once in a while I looked toward Aunty. I was worried about her because of the serious operation she had at the improvised hospital for the Jews. She was still bleeding, but somehow, if one is forced into a situation, one does one's best.

For hours and hours we kept on walking, without any stops, but as long as Aunty was beside me that was all that mattered. With the clean, untouched snow crackling under our feet, we kept up the pace. Finally the soldiers ordered us to take a rest, they could not continue either.

Exhausted, we each sat down on the frozen, snow-covered road, except I used one of my loaves to sit on. I remembered being told, "Better be careful." Our dry and sore throats were wishing for a drink. There was none. So we could not eat either. Even before we realized how good it felt to sit, we were all rounded up to continue our journey. I left the loaf behind.

Night was falling and the soldiers herded us into a farmer's place somewhere in Poland. I could see some of the girls who had taken shelter in a chicken coop drinking all the fresh eggs they could find. I was offered one but could not drink it.

Aunty Sara and I found ourselves in front of a small, lighted house. As we entered the door jammed closed right behind us. There was no room even to drop a pin, but we somehow managed to scoot down and lean against the wall. It was heavenly in the dimly-lit room with a roof above our heads. Only some loud laughter from behind a door disturbed our dozing — a few of the girls had joined the soldiers.

Dawn came too soon. We were all gathered, like the farmer's chickens, without a roll call, to continue our journey.

We walked all day, resting only once. The second night fell as we passed through a village and to our amazement along the edge of the road some tables were set with water and pitchers and cups. We each had a drink, then continued our walk.

Entering a village with all the houses deserted, we were ordered to take shelter wherever we could. The street was also deserted and dark, but some girls were calling out, "There is more room here."

Aunty and I entered a dark place. We were told to climb up and as we were feeling our way a pleasant sensation overcame us. It was fresh smelling straw — finally some softness after all those wooden coyas. We quickly fell asleep.

We felt sorry to leave our warm straw nest but we were also feeling very lucky that all went well the night before, since right in the middle of the upstairs, which was an abandoned mill, there was huge hole where fortunately no one had fallen.

Still holding onto my untouched loaf of bread, my little bandana in which I carefully wrapped the ten dollar bills, and a spoon which served no purpose at the moment, I started to walk beside Aunty. Our pace was getting slower and we found ourselves toward the end of the long line, near collapse.

We tried to hold onto each other for support but it did not help. A gunshot rang out right behind us; a body fell. Aunty grabbed my arm and we started to move toward the middle of the line.

My shoe gave me a big, painful blister on the back of my heel, which made walking a torture until I simply turned the shoe down and walked on it; then it was hard to keep it on.

Aunty and I were fearful of losing speed and finding ourselves again toward the back. We agreed on a manoeuver: walk fast for a while, then stay still in place for a while.

Now our march became a death march. We found ourselves dragging our hungry and dehydrated bodies. For what? To where? Once in a while in the distance a black spot was seen on the white snow. We were certain that there must have been other transports ahead of us and some did not make it. Seemingly fear makes one strong; it certainly did something for us.

Toward the afternoon the scenery changed and we approached a small village. Up till now we had walked with our eyes staring down at the snowy road and so we were surprised to find ourselves in the middle of a street where some people were going about their business. I slowed down for a moment. A fellow with a bayonet gave me a strong shove. Oh how I wished for his death that instant, such a hatred went through me, like never before. But, humiliated, I picked up speed along with Aunty Sara, whose loving smile urged me on. I was glad that even with getting this push I still could stand erect.

The harsh and loud, "Schneller, schneller!" (faster, faster) took us out of the city limits quickly. We continued our walk through frozen fields on each side of the road, fighting for each breath as we stumbled on. Then the girls detected a farmhouse in the distance and a water pump in front of it. Soon they began running toward the pump. How I wished to be able to do the same, but there was no more energy left. I did, however, discover a fresh layer of clean, white snow, took my spoon, and, scooping a spoonful at a time on our way, shared it with Aunty Sara. We felt renewed. I was careful not to overdo eating the snow, since I could hear Granny's voice saying, "If you eat only a little bit it won't hurt you."

The soldiers did not even bother to chase us any longer. It seemed this was the end of the journey and suddenly, after a small hill, there it was, an abandoned railroad station, and our long and exhausting death walk had come to an end. Open cattle cars stood there, waiting for us. We climbed inside and fell to the floor.

We sat silently, together, with the clear, blue, freezing winter sky above us. But as the sky darkened an hysteria of crying broke out and spread like a wild fire. Then the blanket, which hung across the wagon with the soldiers and some girls behind it, was pushed aside and an angry Polish girl started to shout at us. "You fools, you better be quiet and do not aggravate the soldiers any more because they will shoot you down without any warning!"

All eyes looked at each other and Aunty Sara asked timidly, "Is there anyone who can recite the Shema?" a voice answered, "Yes," from the opposite corner. The voice of the wife of the rabbi started us out: "Hear, oh Israel, the Lord is one...." Under the dark sky all the voices joined in and the Shema made us forget our troubles, even though momentarily. Aunty Sara whispered to me that the outbreak of crying was the result of a breakdown in some of those poor souls.

All this praying brought back to me the voice of Granny as she used to recite her evening prayers before she fell asleep and her moidianu lefanecha (morning prayer) before she ate her breakfast, and how upset she was when I missed saying all those short blessings before each food I started to eat. She observed every little ritual she was brought up with, yet for me they were an effort. Times changed and life became hurried; we became less observant of the rituals.

Here and now, however, this solemn prayer brought peace and somehow even death was no threat.

A tiny voice beside Aunty deliriously asked for a drink. The voice kept on repeating, "Water, water..." but no one had any. Others heard her and they also started to ask for water. We were all dehydrated, burning from thirst. We did need water.

Aunty Sara asked the little woman beside her, "Would you drink your own urine?" and the woman said, "Yes!" She tried to urinate but could not. Then Aunty asked me if I could and handed me a small cup. She also suggested that I try it first, but the salty taste made me sick. I handed the cup to the woman. She drank some and closed her eyes.

The anxiety of possible death during our sleep did not let us really relax. The fear that perhaps they would blow us up, wagon and all, haunted us, since we were sitting there and nothing was moving.

I pulled my jacket over my head and fell into a fitful slumber. I tried to change position and some tiny, white and cold snowflakes landed on my face. I pushed back the jacket and found myself all covered with snow. I gave a tiny shove and woke Aunty up, like a child happy to see snow for the first time. It was so close now that it gave me an idea; I took my spoon out and started to eat.

All the girls eagerly scooped up the snow from their coats and blankets. The wagons were still standing immobile, but at least we were alive. Then suddenly a hunger pang hit me. I reached beside me for my loaf of bread, untouched through all our days of walking. It wasn't there. The girl on my left was devouring it and insisted it was hers. She was a big, strong-looking girl with a wild look in her eyes, so I just gave up silently without a fight. I did not want to alarm Aunty, who would have scratched out her eyes for me. I just stared with hatred toward the munching girl. That was the only weapon I had left — hatred. Though before this ordeal I had not hated anything or anyone ever, now, it seemed that hatred made me feel that I accomplished something.

Suddenly the wagon wheels started to roll. All day we rode. Looking up from our open wagons, we could see many fairytale houses, like those in Hansel and Gretel story books, flying by. The clear blue sky was brilliant. We were relieved to have survived another night, to be able to see the wonders and the beauty of life. How we appreciated every day of our life now; life itself was a miracle even though no one knew where these cattle wagons were taking us. Just last night it seemed death was near, yet now, looking at the clear sky, I felt that we would survive.

The cattle cars were speeding now to our new destination, as if someone were chasing us. And in fact they were. We had no idea how fast the Allies were closing in.

Late in the afternoon the wagons stopped and we were taken into a deserted camp with many wooden barracks. Inside, the wooden coyas were unusally clean, which made me wonder about the people who slept or suffered on them. If only they could have talked.

We were at Dachau, West Germany.

Having been rushed away from Auschwitz, Poland with no chance of being liberated, although we did not know this then, it looked as if no one knew what to do with us and so, after the first meager meal in days, we were ordered to continue our walk.

Toward sunset we arrived at and entered a large building. We were ordered to strip again, herded into a hot shower, and then, in an orderly five-abreast column, started to leave the building. We could not see the outside; it was dark by now. "Schneller, schneller!" came the sound of a strong voice I recognized instantly.

I was shaking from excitement but did not want to alert Aunty till I was sure. As I passed the person hurrying us into the dimly-lit hall, I whispered softly,

"Rose?"

The ordering voice stopped; she looked at me and embraced me gently. For a moment happy childhood memories flowed through my veins, our playing together, our double dates, particularly the last one, her with the handsome officer and me with the police chief.

Rose told Aunty and me to step aside and as soon as she was finished she would come and get us. I was so proud to see "one of us" in power!

The waiting seemed endless. Exhausted, dehydrated, and semi-delirious, but fighting till the last drop of blood for our survival, we stood there and waited. Finally Rose came and took us to her barracks, which looked more like a home, with white cement outside walls and many windows.

The room was filled with familiar faces from our home town. Heidy, her mother, her sister, and my cousin with her near-sighted sister whose glasses had been taken — all survived along with many others.

What a reunion that was and how happy I was when Heidy's mother offered us a place beside them. At least with all of us together now it would be easier to wait for the end, whatever it might be.

Next morning, after a short outdoor count, we were assured that there was no crematorium here; a heavy load fell off our chests.

This was Bergen-Belsen.

These pictures were taken by a Marine at the liberation of Auschwitz just hours after our evacuation.

13

Here, with others gathered up at the last minute from all over, there were no regular baths with the chance of being gassed. But a lice epidemic broke out and sickness and malnutrition began to take their deadly toll. Who knows, if one had to choose, what is the best way to die, but this at least was more natural.

Sitting all day on the floor, I started to wonder about certain things. The fear which froze my mind before was gone. Here we felt like one big family. Only one thing was wrong: we had nothing to do. We were too much afraid to plan for survival, our meager diet was rendering us weaker and weaker, and even though we got to sit side by side all day, we had no energy to talk. Rose kept the place clean, the warm sun rays helped, and just sitting with Heidy and not saying a word served to bring a measure of joy for the friendship we had cherished for so many years.

One day Heidy was asked to work in the kitchen, which was behind our sleeping quarters. Most of us were undernourished, helplessly skinny, yet she somehow could retain her well-developed and shapely body, and that was very rare. Also, kitchen help was scarce, and so Heidy accepted the position.

Now she slept away from us, in a privileged kitchen helpers' quarters. This gave us more leg room, which was much needed and appreciated. We still had to sleep feet to feet, packed like sardines. No room was long enough for the number of people packed into it.

A few days passed and Heidy must have been lonely, for she came and asked if I would like to sleep beside her, away from the crowd. That night, sharing one blanket, I could not help but feel her feverishly hot body. I asked her the next morning if she was all right, and she assured me that she was.

One day, she came to share a delicacy with us. First her mother took a bite, then her sister, and then she offered it to me. I politely refused it. I was famished, but just like back home, I would not eat or drink after anyone and so she did not get offended; she remembered that was how I was.

As time went on, the showers were omitted altogether. The Germans had other worries to cope with. The lice infestation grew worse and worse. They invaded our dresses inside the seams and especially our fuzzy new hair. Little by little it got so unbearable that I discarded my underwear and had only one dress on again, just as when we arrived at Auschwitz. This dress was a light flannel one which we had been given upon our arrival at Bergen-Belsen. For some reason the lice did not like it. The cold winter was over and it was easier to cope with life in one dress not liked by lice! Now only my head was a problem.

The sun felt wonderful — it could only mean that it was spring again. But I felt sad. I left last year in spring and found myself here, covered with lice, dying from hunger, in rags, and only skin and bone. I was the little girl who never had to worry, who never did anything wrong, and who always saw life through rose-colored glasses. At any rate, it was easier now among friends and especially with Aunty Sara still beside me.

One night in the peaceful darkness an hysterical cry awoke us. It was one of the twin sisters I knew from back home, very pretty and rather petite. She was pacing the floor, burning with fever. We just looked at her, ourselves helpless and scared. Somehow Rose managed to send for a doctor and much to my surprise I recognized her as she tried to help this poor girl.

She was from a poor family back home and earned her Gymnasium tuition through tutoring. She had tutored one of my friends and me. How proud it made me feel to see her as a doctor, to see her readiness to help, even though it was in the middle of the night. Here we did not fear to report sickness, since there was no crematorium.

When the doctor left she told the other sister, "This is a case of typhoid and only time will heal."

Every morning we still had to stand roll call, but it was not as humiliating and strict, for Rose was our friend.

One morning, as I was standing outside, waiting to be counted, everything turned black in front of my eyes. I fainted and fell to the ground. Aunty trembled, but with the little energy she had left she picked me up and carried me inside. It was typhoid. The burning fever made so many of us so weak that the German women had to come inside to count us.

My health continued to wane. The hearing in my left ear was weaker, my teeth looked huge because the gums were receding, I was skin and bone, and I was covered with lice.

The sad day came again of having to move. This building was to house some fortunate mothers with their babies, who were saved at the last minute by coming here instead of Auschwitz. It was heart-warming to see a few live children and also some Hungarian women with their long hair.

In our new place, among strange people and with new Polish girls in charge, we were deprived of Rose's special concern. The quarters of the supervisor, shared with her crew, seemed again plentifully supplied and once in a while they discarded some potato peelings, which were rapidly gobbled up by the ones still able to fight. Our meals diminished to nothing — a turnip daily was our only sustenance. People suffered from dehydration, diarrhea and starvation. Disease was spreading over us like a deadly blanket. There was no refuge or hideaway; we were all being swallowed up one way or the other and all we could do was just to sit and wait for our turn. The only thing most of us still had left was the will to survive. But some did not want to live. Each morning their dead bodies were carried outside.

On my left sat two sisters with whom I went to the Lyceum. I remembered how one day they took me home to meet their father, a dentist, and their strict mother, whom I did not exactly admire. The younger sister was rapidly fading away, though we all tried to encourage her to hold on. Her only response was, "I know my parents are dead and I do not want to live without them." Next morning her stiff body was taken and the following day her sister's. Now I was determined never to say, "I don't want to live."

The pile of cold, stiff bodies outside along the building grew taller and taller each day. It had a definite shape, with the bodies crisscrossed over each other. Aunty told me that she read somewhere in a book how dead bodies were piled up in this shape, she called it "gleda," and then set on fire. Each day on our way to the outdoor latrine, the horrifying sight confronted us. We shivered at the thought that perhaps we would also wind up on top of this pile.

One day I woke up with the pain and discomfort of diarrhea and although I did not want to, I made my way to the primitive outdoor bathroom. It was a huge, round and deep hole, dug out and framed with some heavy logs on which one was lucky to balance without falling.

As I moved toward the door to go outside I had to step over the girls all stretched out on the floor. One had only a cavity where her nose should be, yet she was still breathing, her eyes still open. It gave me such a shock that I almost fainted. How deep we had sunk. Why couldn't we rather die to omit this last painful and inhuman chaos? I was shaken by sadness and also by anger. Where was the world we had left behind and all the people in it? But there was no answer and if one wanted to live, one could, and I somehow still wanted to.

A sad and begging cry awoke us one night. I opened my eyes and under the soft moonlight which fell on the wooden floor I could see a woman's body with its outstretched arms begging for water. She probably was deported with the last Hungarian transports, as her head was not shaved. Fiery red, wavy hair framed her ashen face. We all felt so sorry but were helpless and the next morning when I went outside, her body was on top of the pile of dead, her beautiful red hair hanging over the other dead bodies.

I wondered who she was. Perhaps she was a performer of some kind, as she begged for water so graciously, and even now, on top of the pile, she looked beautiful. I trembled at the depth of my anger at this senseless torture which was inflicted upon us innocent ones.

Our water supply ended, we were forbidden to leave our room, and all we had now was one turnip, first to be shared among four, then among more and more until it became impossible to share it equally. The divided pieces were very small yet it was a hardship to chew them.

A small, dried, hard-like-a-rock piece of bread, which I had found after the two sisters were evacuated from the room, was my daily delight. I could not eat it but I sucked on it a little bit each day. Even though I had to first scrape off the mold, it tasted wonderful, that piece of long-forgotten bread. Each day I would neatly tuck it away till the next.

We were sitting and disintegrating inch by inch. Outside, spring was teasing us through the windows. The lice got worse but it made me nauseous to kill them, so I took advantage of Aunty and after I combed my head she would smash the lice one by one. This was our daily routine, the only routine.

As I lay silently in a daze, weak and famished after almost a week without food or water, a terrible thirst came over me. Just like the last flickers of a burned-out candle I was without enough energy even to speak. Yet a faint voice came out of me asking for water. It seemed a hopeless request for Aunty was also fading beside me. But she heard me, got up and disappeared.

The small container in her outstretched hand must has elicited some pity from the girls in the kitchen for they filled the cup with water. When she poured it down my throat I opened my eyes for a second to show my gratitude, then fell back into a semi-coma. I did not hear; nothing was hurting. A complete, satisfying, dark feeling came over me.

Was this death?

14

The room was deathly silent. One could not hear a sound or a breath. Suddenly, shooting, running and shouting woke us from our dark solitude. For a moment I felt annoyed to be disturbed but then the door flung open and the smiling face of a soldier with a beret looked inside.

No, this was not a German soldier, for he spoke English. I could see him fighting to control the horror in his voice at the sight which confronted him. Then a few more soldiers came. One soldier came to me, lifted my head gently and gave me a drink. With my eyes closed, I just let it happen. I was afraid to open my eyes and find out that it was a wishful dream. From a deep, dark and peaceful death, I was being rekindled, like a fanned spark.

After a while the soldiers came back with hot chocolate and told us not to eat or drink anything from the premises because all the food and water had been poisoned and kept ready for us. The Germans had been surprised by this attack and so we were saved from the poisoning.

Now we understood the meager turnip a day!

Lying on the floor and daring to live again, all we could do was to wait and have patience for just a little longer. Through the low windows filled with the spring sunshine, which was darkened once in a while by haystack wagons filled up to the top with stiff and cold cadavers, we could see the German men and women cleaning up the aftermath of their inhuman acts.

I witnessed a drastic role change as the murderers, the ones who took the law into their own hands, were being punished, having to pile the corpses onto wagons and then run after them. I should have enjoyed this punishment and hated them, happy that they were getting what they deserved, but I could not. All I wanted was to live and forget.

After the grounds were cleaned, the soldiers carried some of us outside to be kissed by the warm rays of the spring sun, and we realized that yes, we were alive and it was truly spring again.

It was the spring of 1944 when we were torn away, our warm and precious family lives destroyed, and now it was the spring of 1945 in Bergen-Belsen, a hell of lice, sickness and death.

A few days went by and I decided to look for the washroom. As I entered, a horrifying face with two dark eyes deep inside a skull, perched on a skeleteon body covered only with a thin skin, stared at me.

This was the first time in a year that I had seen a mirror. I quickly fled from the room, promising myself to eat, to get fat and not to be picky like before.

With every day we felt more and more alive and tried not to think about how close we had been to death. I survived with Aunty Sara at my side and even though the fresh wounds deep inside were hurting, our will to go on and start to live again like normal human beings was surfacing.

The thick hard shell I had built around myself would have to give way to feelings of love and trust once more. My childhood memories were inside me and would support me. My beautiful past was the only treasure they, the murderers, could not take from me!

Fresh, clean clothes were given out and toiletries, among them sanitary napkins which we would not need for many months yet to come. All the little things in life meant so much now, to feel as a human, having human needs and not to be erased from this earth because of the accident of our birth.

"Attention! Attention!" someone called. It was not a roll call, only a message for the ones who wished to be registered to return to wherever they had come from.

Girls started to walk toward the registration table and I urged Aunty to come with me. Our legs were still weak, but slowly we made it. A person behind the table gave us a small card and our name was given back to us. From that day we were called by our names — we had become persons again. It seemed as if our humanity, of which the Germans had tried to strip us, had been given back and we were on our way to recuperation.

We found ourselves on the other side of Bergen-Belsen, where we had not been before. We had not walked very far when Aunty and I fell from exhaustion. I wondered, "Where does one get energy to do something?" Then I recalled from the past year's experience that if the reason is survival, then one somehow finds the strength that is needed.

In this chaos of liberation we were on our own. Aunty and I found shelter inside a wooden barn where we nestled down in a corner. The place was filled with girls and most of them could walk and look out for themselves. All that the two of us could do was watch in silence and be a little envious.

Dinner time came and the room emptied — everybody went to fetch their supper. Aunty never complained till now, but I could see that she was near the end of her strength. I got up, mustering all the energy I could, and joined the long waiting-line outside. The last rays of the afternoon sun were still above us, but suddenly everything turned dark in front of my eyes. I collapsed and fell to the ground. A girl helped me up and walked me back to the resting place, where Aunty was waiting with a disturbed and hopeless look on her face. I had tried but now we knew that the two of us needed help.

Later a girl brought us our supper. We were very thankful for we could not imagine such kindness. Just a few days ago some would have killed for this food. How fast human actions change, I thought to myself. I started to hope that, after all, there would be more of this kindness to prove to me that it is circumstances which change our actions and somewhere in the world things would be better.

Aunty Sara seemed to be giving up. I pretended

that if she had survived the hell we had been in, she must hold on for a while longer. I did not know how I could cope with more sorrow and pain. I recalled her telling me that all she wanted was to stand beside me, to save me during these horrible times because she felt that she owed this to my Mother, since she was lost because of Aunty's children. All this time she had been brave, encouraging me, and keeping me alive. Now, when we could start living again she was not able to suppress her illness any longer. It was my turn now to care for her.

Then the miracle happened. I opened my eyes one morning and was greeted by the red hair and smiling, hazel-brown eyes of Rose. She had been told about us and she had come to help. In a short while two stretchers took us to a makeshift hospital. This was a clean but small building with many fresh-smelling beds side by side. I was sure that nothing but good things could happen to us now.

We ate and slept and rested and after a few days I developed an interest in going outside to explore. Aunty was very proud of me and that made me even stronger. I was stumbling like a baby who takes its first steps, but I was longing for the warm sunshine which I loved so much.

Each time I returned Aunty began preparing me for the future, but she never included herself. I tried to ignore this. Secretly, deep inside, I was wondering, how does one know about dying? I had been weak and ruined, yet after being rekindled I got energy somehow to want to go on. How come some did not have the same energy? I never argued with her about it. Only once I insisted that she should accompany me outside so I could show her my secret little bush in which I hid in my loneliness and embarrassment about the condition of my body.

As we were lying under the bush on our backs, admiring the clear blue sky and letting only our legs bask in the sun, a truck loaded with soldiers stopped and took pictures. This made us hurry inside and back into our beds. Every morning as we opened our eyes the first thing was to see if we were alright, but we never talked about it.

One day, cousin Irene came to visit and told me that Heidy was dead. I looked at her with dry eyes, but a crying heart. After she left I wondered how I, the girl who cried at the slightest thing, now, when my best and dearest friend departed, had no tears. I was frozen — my emotions, my love, my comprehension. I was still afraid to let go; I was still fighting to survive. That night, however, my pillow was drenched with quiet tears.

Heidy died of tuberculosis I was told. I thought of the night, sleeping beside her and asking her about her feverish body. It had not seemed natural. All the past beautiful days we spent together since we were little girls had now died with her. Only the memories remained. Now, I had no friend. I made myself stop thinking.

One day we were told that a French nurse would come around asking our needs and my mind was feverishly occupied to remember how to ask for a piece of soap and some perfume. My poor French now became almost non-existent since my rusty brain was not working well in any language. It exhausted me completely, thinking all day and trying to remember what I would have been able to recall immediately back home. It also brought a smile to my face as I thought, "Here I am, hardly over the twilight zone, and all I desire are some things for my vanity."

Aunty continued to fade before my eyes, but I refused to see it. She was emphasizing each day that I was never to return to my birthplace, Sighet (Romanian spelling). She did not have to go into details but she made me determined to take her advice.

One day, applications were taken for those who wished to return to their homeland or who wanted to go to Sweden. Aunty, without any hesitation, signed me up on the Swedish list and I relied on her decision. I did not ask questions, I just hoped all would end well. My brain could not have come to an important decision like that, a decision which turned out to be the most fortunate turning point of my life. (I did not know until later that Aunty did not register herself for any transfer.)

A messenger came into our room asking for Aunty Sara. We all looked up curiously. The messenger had been sent by Uncle Joel. The man told us that Uncle Joel also survived in a nearby lager and after the war had been searching near and far till he found us. He would come tomorrow to see us.

Aunty and I could hardly believe it. It was a miracle that he had found us and I knew he was a strong man and that he would take good care of us. Now I could relax. We were in good hands. Aunty asked me to go to the washroom and turn on some of the shower heads. She explained that she was having difficulty urinating and the sound might help her. I followed her orders, turning on all the showers, but nothing happened. I ran around the building asking someone to call a doctor. I did not tell Aunty about it. Soon a group of men and women came and stood consulting around her bed, then left without giving her any medication or the promise of some. I started to quiver with fear.

I went to my bed and closed my eyes. After a few minutes I looked in Aunty's direction and saw her fingers motioning me to come closer. Like being shot from a canon I jumped out of bed. For the first time I was allowing myself to be confronted with her poor condition. I sat down on the edge of her bed. Aunty wanted to say something. I bent over her and started to count desperately so she would not stop breathing. Aunty tried to follow the rhythm. I was counting and counting and did not even realize that she was lying there quietly, her eyes closed. By now, I was exhausted and lying flat over her cold body. Somebody literally peeled me off Aunty's dead body. I fought. I did not want to let go but in shock, finally I was put to bed. I must have passed out because all is black in my memory. I do not remember seeing her body being removed or how I got into bed.

Next morning, unaware of Aunty's death, I opened my eyes and the first thing I did was look toward her bed to say good morning. A strange face looked back at me. The tears started to flow. My heart felt broken, lonely and forlorn. How could I go on without her, without a Mother, no one to comfort me or guide me through this big, wide world full of strangers? I knew how unfortunate some girls were all this time without anyone beside them, but Aunty Sara was my guide, my second mother and my savior. Losing her now seemed almost more than I could bear.

Uncle Joel appeared in the doorway, smiling. I passed out. When I opened my eyes I felt his hands gently stroking my forehead and heard him murmur, "My poor child, my poor child, how sorry I am to be late and miss this reunion."

Tears were flowing down his thin, sad face. Only yestereday the messenger told him how much he was expected by both of us and today all he found was his wife's empty bed.

For a moment I thought he would faint, but he leaned against the doorpost and burst out in bitter crying. After he caught his breath he turned to me, slipped off his wristwatch and told me to hold onto it till he would come back after me.

He never came back.

15

One morning I was moved from this room, full of Aunty's memories which I lived over and over, into a real hospital in Bergen-Belsen, one which had been formerly used for the German soldiers. This new place was well-equipped, in a beautiful setting of lush green lawns.

The dreadful looking faces filling the long narrow room were scary but I looked just like them. The white metal beds were squeezed tightly together. On each footboard hung a medical history. After a couple of days I decided I must get out of bed for a while. My card revealed that I had water spots on my lung. I also heard from the others that many had tuberculosis, but my case was not as serious.

Some of the girls in the next room had no beds — they were on stretchers ready to be wheeled out. They were dying, but at least had the pleasure of one last look at warm, sunny days and beautiful surroundings.

There was plenty of food. Each day a delicious

plate full was brought but I could not eat. I tried to force myself but the look of food made me nauseous. Also, at home each serving was on a different plate and here all the food came on one. Old habits die hard.

One day cousin Irene stood at my bed. She asked me if I was eating right. I started to complain about how heavy the silverware felt, how hard the bed was, etc. etc. Next day, she gave me a tiny set of silver — a spoon and a fork. When the meal came later I found myself at least poking around at it because of the tiny silverware.

After a few days I decided to take a walk. My bony legs could barely carry me, but I headed toward a luscious green field on the horizon. It was a brilliant, sunny day with a clear blue sky. I approached a bench and almost collapsed on it. These few steps were too much but I was so happy to be alive and let the sun warm my bones. Deep in my own reverie I did not realize that someone had sat down beside me.

A young man, kind of grayish and broken-looking, said softly, "Good morning, Lucy. Are you Lucy?" I looked at him and acknowledged that he was right. He told me how often he used to pass my window at home and had stopped to listen to me playing the piano. The fact that he was embarrassed by what he saw in front of him now could not be hidden. I could see it on his face and it made me also terribly embarrassed. His confession brought tears to my eyes, even though I never knew him back home. This complete stranger had revived some lovely memories. I wanted to thank him for remembering me and I wanted to say so much more but I just sat there, sad and embarrassed about my deteriorated self.

The wounds deep inside were very painful and every time I wanted to talk to someone I just broke out crying, so the only way out for the time being was to keep silent and guard my pain.

I weighed less than 50 pounds. I had one inch of hair on my head and my legs and arms were covered with parchment-like skin. My mind was blank much of the time. I felt no particular pain or happiness. I just seemed to walk with open but sightless eyes. There were no more roll calls, no more selections, only a deep, dark empty sleep without dreams. My solitude was my refuge and I chose to be alone.

One morning we were told to get ready, for the Swedish Red Cross was coming to pick us up for the journey across the ocean. There was nothing I had to do to be ready. I had only the nightgown I was wearing and the American money. In the bustle I even lost my favorite little silverware. All they had to carry was my skeleton.

This was my first ocean voyage. I remembered having studied about oceans, but I had never seen one. As I was looking through the tiny porthole from my top bunk, a panorama spread out before me — the wavy ocean and the sunset. It was breathtaking to witness this huge red ball of fire, slowly getting smaller and smaller, taking a shape of a perfect cup and saucer, then slowly disappearing. It excited me so that I felt the blood pounding in my temples. I had always admired nature. The beauty and mystery kept me in suspense and now all I wished was that my other secret dreams which had kept me alive would come true — to find Zoli, who supposedly was in Spain, and to find a man and romance and to be able to raise a family of my own.

Our next stop was in a railroad station where they placed me on a stretcher. I could see a high glass dome which covered the entire waiting hall. The noise of the rushing trains and the harsh sound of the whistles lingered on in my ears for many years. The terrible loud sounds trapped underneath the dome, I found out a year later, had destroyed my hearing in one ear.

There were many, many stretchers placed side by side as we waited for the next move. Pretty Swedish nurses were buzzing around us with their happy smiles, curtsying in response to the compliments they received from their superiors. That brought a smile to my tired lips. As children we also had to curtsy, but not as adults.

It was nice to see smiles and happiness again. It reminded me of my rich and beautiful childhood. I started to get curious to see this country which was now my new home.

We were loaded on the trains and next day arrived in Helsingborg, Sweden. It was summer 1945.

After many hours of disinfecting and cleaning we were taken to a schoolhouse converted into a hospital. I was beginning to feel human in my clean clothes, donated by the Red Cross.

The huge building was full, with beds in every room. I chose a corner bed beside a huge window. All I wanted was privacy and to be able to look outside.

One morning as I was lying on the bed, like a flash of lightning, Zoli's address came to me. I never had to address an envelope at home yet the vision of my Mother's handwriting came back to me: "L'hopital d'Optalmoligique, Spain." I called the nurse and begged her to bring me a pencil and paper. My fingers could not hold the pencil so she helped me.

The torture of trying to hold a pencil did not compare to the torture of trying to concentrate. My brain was burning and my heart pounding as I put a few words together. Little by little I found myself writing about Mother, how I hoped to find her soon and how happy we would all be together again. I went on and on, feverishly, not realizing the extent of my missplaced enthusiasm. The nurse addressed the envelope and mailed it.

Only when, by some miracle, an answer came from Zoli and there was no mention of Mother did a terrible shock and shame come over me. I wanted to reply but it took a long time before I had the nerve to write again. Mother was never again mentioned and that was even worse. I remembered his love for Mother. His ambition to become a doctor was only to make her proud of him, and I also remembered Zoli promising Mother that when I grew up he would send me to Switzerland to a famous all-girl institute. Now I was alone, and he was in Spain, so far away, but at least one of my dreams had come true — I had found my brother.

Everyday life went on, seemingly peaceful. The sick and the tired ones stayed in bed most of the time, but the more energetic began to go about their business again.

One afternoon a nurse announced that a famous make-up manufacturer had sent us some gifts. We all jumped out of bed and I think I was the first one to stand in front of the table loaded with make-up, combs and powder cases. My eyes could not believe that all these beautiful things were here simply for the taking.

Searching carefully through the pile, I selected a gold-plated compact with a tiny lipstick in the side of it and one small ruby on its end. I thanked the nurses and went back to bed where I carefully placed the treasure under my pillow. I guarded it with my life yet never used it.

One morning as I was sitting on the window sill, basking in the sun, a tiny face stared back at me. It scared me to see the exact image of my brother Zoli reflected in the window — a head covered with very short dark hair and two round brown eyes. Quickly I withdrew and each morning following I sat in the warm sun with my eyes closed.

A nurse approached me one day asking if I would be willing to accept a gift of fresh fruits. I looked at her in surprise. She pointed across the street to what seemingly was an orchard. When she returned with a basketfull of fruit I so much wanted to ask her to thank the person responsible and to let them know how much I appreciated their gesture, but all I did was smile and accept the basket. I hoped she could see the appreciation on my face and reflected in my eyes.

As word spread around the town about us, people of all ages came to get a glimpse. Even though we were high up on the second floor of the building, they would patiently stand on the sidewalk below, trying to question us about our past experience. Some found it hard to believe the things they heard. Some spoke German, some French, and they all seemed very emotional after we answered their questions. The one thing which made them believe us was our skeletal-like bodies. Some asked us to come down to the playground of the school and they took pictures of us. They were nice enough to give us some copies. Then I really could see myself!

A certain group of youngsters became our daily visitors. They were light-complexioned with shiny straw-blond hair. To show us how they felt about us, since they did not speak our language nor we theirs, they formed a straight line and with their hands inside their jackets imitated the heart beating. Yes, we did get the message and it made us feel good to see their compassion. One day the nurse brought me a small note from one of the boys asking if I needed anything. I asked her to tell him, not right now, but I would think about it.

Now as each day passed, my energy came back, my weight increased and I found myself taking short walks. One day as I walked down the corridor, much to my surprise, I discovered a piano in the corner. What a beautiful sight! It seemed as if this old, scarred piano was calling me. My heart started to beat faster, my feet almost running toward it. I sat down on the bench and cried. I remembered our grand piano, the "friend" I grew up with, and who comforted me all my life, taking the beatings according to my moods. But now, as I looked at this keyboard, I could not move. I stared for a while then slowly placed my bony fingers on the keys. I could not remember any music; my mind was like a blank page. It was as if I had never played, ever. I sat there a long time and recalled how I used to dream in Auschwitz about a favorite music piece and tried to practice it in my memory. My fingers started to move.

The nurse heard me from her office and came over. She reminded me about the young Swedish boy's offer. Now I knew what I needed — music, lots and lots of music and especially one piece: Liszt's Second Hungarian Rhapsody. I had just been starting to learn this piece when we were uprooted from our home.

How happy I was the next day when the nurse came running and brought me the requested music. I in return sent him a round and very thin aluminum medal on which I scratched my name and my thanks. I had nothing of real value to give in exchange for his kindness, but it made me feel good to know that this small gift would remind him of the brief moments we had spent looking at each other from the window sill. Now that the piano was drawing out my human feelings once more, I felt I would at last like to find a girlfriend to talk to. I started to look around the room, really for the first time. I discovered a lonely-looking girl with a pale face, lying on her pillow. I approached her and asked her if she would mind talking to me. She looked up sadly and tried to smile. That made me feel welcome and I sad on her bedside asking her about her plans. No one ever talked about the hell of this last year. It was as if it had never happened. We kept it inside of us and hoped that time would heal our souls.

This girl was an uneducated Jewish girl. Suddenly I felt the challenge to make a lady out of her. Was this how Mother used to feel? I plunged myself into telling her all about the society I grew up in, the schools, the small jours (parties), my friends. And as I was going on and on it brought me back from the world in which I had been for one long year. The memories just kept pouring out, endlessly. She listened silently to every word I said and I could see a tiny flicker of hope in her gray eyes. She told me, "You are a good story-teller and it makes me forget my aches and pains."

One day, when I had learned a bit of Swedish, the nurse told me that soon we would have to leave. This time I was prepared and not afraid, though I was very disappointed about having to miss our daily visitors, the young boys who so faithfully came to serenade us.

Before our last day I asked permission to go downstairs and walk in the garden. My friend and I got dressed. She put a dress on, but I was too conscious of my skinny legs, so I left my pyjama pants on underneath my coat. Since it was around the time when the boys were used to coming, they discovered us behind the fence and took pictures. Soon they came running back with copies to give us, almost like they knew this would be the last time together.

I wrote quickly to Zoli about our change again and how good it felt this time that from now on we would know about each other's whereabouts. We still had to find Oscar. I completely stopped writing about Mother, yet wherever I went I kept on searching for her face. This silent quest did not stop for a very long time after the war.

The arrival at the new destination was disappointing. This school was an older building, cold, and it came like a shock. I found myself in a room with all Polish-speaking girls and immediately the aroma of their cooking in the corridors almost drove me insane. The aroma reminded me of Granny's cooking back home and how her effort was wasted on Oscar and me. We never appreciated food, yet somehow at this place all I had to feed on was new and strange dishes with their strange aromas. It was surely a healthful diet we were being fed by the hospital but these girls insisted on cooking other things on a small burner in the hallways. To me, it was all strange.

On my right lay an older Polish woman with an angry, green face. She never talked to me. On my left was a young, pretty girl with her old mother. This girl complained night and day and the poor old mother had to suffer it all. At times she would look over to my bed and point out my good behaviour to her daughter, which made the girl even more angry.

As I was looking at my powder compact one day, the green-faced Polish woman on my right saw it and forthrightly asked me to give it to her. I didn't give it to her, but the next day the tiny jewelled lipstick was gone. I cried. I recalled again all the lovely things I left behind. This one more would only add to the list.

After a short stay at this place the girls started to show obvious symptoms of disease. We were still without any medication. The water spots on my lungs did not develop further, but some girls were dying and others were moved to a different wing.

One day, Kornbarum Juci, a very prominent girl from my home town, came to my bed and asked if I would go with her and try to convince her sick little sister to survive. They had been in Auschwitz with their mother, who had died there, and now the little sister did not want to live.

We entered a large room with many beds and from one of them a pair of feverish black eyes stared at me. The bushy, black hair around her tiny face scared me for a moment and I wanted to run, but the older sister said to her, "Can you see? There are other girls looking like you. Skeletons!" She pointed to me. "Yet they want to live and get well!" The words seemed to bounce right off the little sister. The next day she died.

Above: Bertil Swenson, who sent the copy of Liszt's Second Hungarian Rhapsody. Left: My first steps in the schoolyard (with my pyjama bottoms on); Halsingborg, Sweden, 1945.

Split picture of group in Halmstad, 1945. First person seated on left took my jewelled lipstick. I am fourth from the left, standing, with my favorite nurse fifth from left.

First on right on the floor is the girl who always
complained. Her mother is seated on her right.

16

One day, a tall, slender, graying Swedish woman came into our room. She had warm eyes and a smile on her small round face. She looked us over then left. Later the nurse came and fetched me and another girl from the room. In our robes, we followed her till we were standing face to face with an angelic-looking Swedish lady. She took us under our arms, realizing our weak and unstable walk, and pointed us toward a room. There was a gray-haired gentleman, her husband, waiting for us. They explained, in German, that they did not have children and since they loved children so much they would like to help us. It was a very strenuous conversation for all of us.

Back in my room, a nurse brought me a box full of mouth-watering delicacies. There were a couple of fresh eggs, different cheeses, a chunk of butter, fruits, and a piece of homemade Swedish coffee cake. From that day on the box came regularly once a day.

After a few weeks, as I got acquainted with the

nurse, I asked her if she knew anything about American currency. I told her about my good fortune in Auschwitz and that after all this time of fearful hiding I was still in possession of some bills. I told her about how I used to pass the showers, even selections, with the bills folded inside my mouth. The nurse's big round eyes opened wider and my confession scared even me.

After consulting with the caring Swedish lady, Gurli Anderson, the nurse took me to the bank. I had no idea if what I had kept hidden was real money until I found myself holding a stack of kronor in my hand. This Swedish money was also strange to me.

On the way back to the hospital, a beautiful pair of black, shiny rubber boots caught my attention. I purchased them and have them to this day. I will never part with them. I also chose some fabric for a new wardrobe. Even though I had never learned to sew at home (it was a poor girls' trade) my first desire was to start sewing as soon as I would be able to sit up long enough.

One day we were surprised by a visitor from Helsingborg. He was a tall, slender man who could not speak our language but was there every day. He asked for permission for my friend and me to go downstairs with him. There he had us sit on a bench, with him in the middle, and started to open a box. It contained two dresses, one for each of us, and some carefully wrapped homemade pastries. Not much was said but we sat there side by side, looking at each other and smiling. With sign language he talked about the group of young boys who also had been our daily visitors in Helsingborg. He told us that they had come to see us here but had not been allowed to enter the school grounds.

They were told we were quarantined because of TB. This made me furious, not to be able to see those sun-shiny faces and and to know that they had been turned back after so long a journey. But, we were refugees and so could not change anything.

I wrote to my brother Zoli about the lovely Swedish couple, Gurli and Aldor Anderson, who were showing so much love to us. He wrote them, thanking them for their kindness. Aunty Gurli and Uncle Aldor, as we learned to call them, came running one day with the French-written letter for me to translate. It was one of the happiest days we ever spent together.

As time went on our friendship grew deeper. I started to explore my feelings toward them — they wanted to experience the love of children, but where was my love? The love for my Mother, yes, I could feel that, but after the many disappointing and unfortunate past experiencees I was finding it difficult to open up to others. The pain was too fresh and I knew love could hurt me if I let it. I was fighting against any attach-ments by reasoning that they were at best only tempo-rary and therefore relatively meaningless.

Aunt Gurli and Uncle Aldor knew my religion and identity and wanted to talk about my past, always assuring me that I should be proud of it. But their concern was of no avail — I still felt hunted, hurt and frightened. What gems these two people were — how many people like them were to be found in all the world? — but I was like a newborn. I needed to learn all over to live, to love, to trust. My wish to survive was fulfilled. Now it was time to be strong, to do the right things and to find the right place in life. That would not be such an easy task. I didn't know if I was up to it.

Winter was in the air once more and we had to leave, to make room for the school children. Now I was convinced that when I decided not to open my heart to these lovely people I had done the right thing. I had to leave them behind and I told myself they were just another sad episode added to the rest. I cried, they cried, and the train rushed out of the station.

The ride was not long but it was late in the afternoon when we arrived at our new destination. A tall, dark-haired nun, with her long navy cape wrapped around her, was waiting for us. She ordered a few taxis and we were taken to a convalescent home up on a hill on the outskirts of a small town. It was a two-story, warm and brightly-lit building. We each got to choose a room which we shared with two other girls.

One of my roomates was a woman in her late thirties, neat and well put together, who spoke with well-chosen words. The other one was a tall young girl in her early twenties with a large head and bushy black hair and a fun-loving attitude. It was the beginning of a beautiful friendship.

A bell was heard and door after door opened as we all headed for the dining hall, a large, softly-lit room with white tablecloths. What a sight! In the back was a long table set with food. I was in line with my plate when all at once an arm flung around me and a voice exclaimed how good it was to see me. I turned to see one of the girls who had worked for Aunty Sara in her craft shop. She had helped support her parents by sewing beautiful needlepoint tapestries and later took over the store in Aunty's absence. What warm memories flooded my cold heart.

One morning we were taken to a warehouse and got to select to our hearts' content all the winter clothes we needed. I selected the necessities, and then asked if I could also have a ski outfit and boots. My wish was granted and I walked away ecstatic with my selections. No one else picked a ski outfit as most of the girls were from poor, working families and did not know of such pleasures as skiing. Now I started to plan for the future — there was a chance of some fun and I wanted to prepare for it.

A most beautiful sight greeted me the next day as I looked out the window — glittering white snow covered the hills, the roads and my window sill. This snow brought joy and anticipation, not like before on our walk from Auschwitz to Bergen-Belsen. Outside, Sister Martha brought me a sled, a most unusual one that looked like a low chair mounted onto two metal bars. I stood in the back of it on the bars and let the slope of the hills carry me to bottom. What a sensation!

One day a letter came from America. It was from Father's brother, Uncle Joe. I remembered his faithful correspondence with my Mother and once in a while a package with special gifts. He had urged Father to leave everything behind and come to America as the times got harder and harder. I recalled the discussions between Father and Mother about this, but as human nature was, and is, they kept on hoping for a turn for the better. How I wished at this moment that I could have convinced them to leave all their past behind and go where a new life would have saved them, but I was too young then and did not dare to air my views. A handful of my home town people did quietly disappear, but most of us let ourselves be herded, like animals, into a slaughter house, willingly submitting, it seemed, to the slaughter. Except for me, the slaughter was instead a lengthy torture and humiliation almost worse than death itself.

A large package arrived from Uncle Joe. All the relatives who lived in New York had put together some clothes and among them, much to my surprise, were a couple boxes of chocolates. What a delight! I shared some of the dresses with girls who were the right size for them and offered my roommates some of the chocolate-covered filberts. The rest I placed on my night stand — the sight of them alone satisfied me.

The girls up and down the hall were so happy to wear American dresses. The neighbor girl next door seemed especially pleased. She was in her late twenties, with red curly hair and matching eye balls, huge feet and clumsy arms hanging at her sides. She told us how the Germans performed a certain operation on her. She did not reveal the details, but her deep, manly voice left little to our imaginations.

The building a few feet away housed two sets of mothers with their daughters and some German-speaking women and men from Austria. They kept to themselves and most of us who spoke Hungarian kept to ourselves. One day, though, I found a piano and began to go every day to practise the music the Swedish boy from Helsingborg had given me. Among the small group from the other building were a German-speaking brother and sister, both middle-aged, very thin and with rather grayish complexions. They seemed refined and seldom mixed with the others. One evening, while walking back from our supper, I heard a voice behind me exclaim, "She has the most beautifully-shaped legs!" I had heard such comments back home, but coming from this usually silent, middle-aged gentleman it was something special. I shyly turned and smiled, acknowledging his compliment.

After a few days passed he approached me and asked if I would accompany him on the violin which he played only secretly, never in front of a crowd. He suggested we meet in the dining room where there was also a piano. He saw the frightened look on my face and quickly made it clear that Sister Martha's quarters were right above the dining room. I wanted to make it clear to him that that was my secondary concern — the first being that I did not think I was an accompanist and even the thought of it scared me. However, since I could not speak the German language enough to explain this, I agreed to meet him at 8 o'clock that evening.

He was already there when I entered the dining room. He pointed me toward the piano and I obediently walked over to it. I sat down quietly. We did not speak. Then he started to play his violin softly and so professionally that I almost fainted from happiness. The notes in front of me, like magic, just flowed in rhythm. What a thrill!

After we finished the concerto he closed the book, thanked me and suggested that it was my bedtime. I could have played all night but like an obedient child I started to walk with him toward my complex. When we arrived he kissed my hand and bade me goodnight. After that, he barely acknowledged me, or anyone else for that matter, and went back to his withdrawn silence, like one who had used all his energy in one all-consuming task.

Spring came and the narrow, unpaved road winding down to town became dry and nice for walking. Our first adventure out from our hideaway took us to many nice shops, all filled with beautiful clothes and shoes. Everything looked so tempting, but we had no money. As we were walking and admiring the rich and glamorous windows I came face to face with Lisetta, the girl from Auschwitz. Now she was all alone — her mother and little sister had died back on the roads somewhere. We embraced and parted.

My two roommates and I became very dependent on each other. Ella, the eldest one, kept us in suspense with her past marital experiences. Sue was a great comedienne. She also sang beautifully and our theme song was chosen: Avant de Murir (Before Death). I played the piano and she sang, till one day she became ill, was taken to a hospital and died soon after. I never played the piece again.

One day a man came taking photographs for people to send to their family and friends who survived. Everybody was anxious for their pictures to be taken, but my friend Ella and I stayed in the background. The man offered us a free picture. From then on we became good friends. Since Ella knew German, the two of them had long conversations which I was able only to partially understand. He had survived Dachau and, like others, was struggling to find his way back to love and trust.

When the time came for all the girls in the home to move on, he proposed to me. Among hundreds of available girls, I was the chosen one; our attraction had been mutual right from the beginning. Even though I really did not know him or anything of his past, I accepted him unconditionally and knew that this could be a partner for a lifetime. My intuition was correct. My husband, Hugo, became a guardian angel and soul supporter to me.

Now two of my wishes had come true. I had found my brother Zoli and I had found a man with whom I could share my life.

Hugo and I became husband and wife, December 1946.

Left: Lisetta, middle, whom I met "out of the ashes" on an Alingsas, Sweden street.

Right: My dear roomate, Susan, who died still in possession of her engagement ring which survived the Holocaust.

Left: Performing an Hungarian folk dance (csardas) at the Alingsas, Sweden convalescent home in 1945.

Right: The woman seated choreographed the International Musical Event and made my csardas costume.

Ahlefors, Sweden, 1945. At front are the
two sisters who recognized me upon arrival.

The author with roomate,
Susan.

Above: A good friend from Goteborg came to visit us in Halmstad, against quarantine rules.

With roommate, Ella.

Hugo's sister, Irma, and husband, Lothar Tauber from Brno, Czechoslovakia. Does anyone know their whereabouts?

My guardian angel, Gurli
Anderson,   on the way to the bank.

Pictures with my friends
before ex changing the $10 bills.

My guardian angels, Gurli and Aldor Anderson.
Halmstad, Sweden, 1945.

Uncle Joe, New York, 1946.

Afterword

Alice immigrated with her husband, Hugo Kern, to the United States in 1948.

In Portland, Oregon, they raised four beautiful daughters. After they all were married, the Kerns decided to retire in Palm Springs, California. There they became members of Temple Isaiah, led by Rabbi Joseph Hurwitz. Mrs. Kern is a past Sisterhood President of Temple Isaiah and B'nai B'rith Women. Her writings include a book of poems and songs. She also conducts a volunteer choir and is president of the Holocaust Survivors of the Desert.

Alice Kern has told her story on radio, television, in Sunday School and public school classes and before civic groups. She is available to share her story and may be contacted through the Holocaust Resource Center, Portland, Oregon.

* Tattooed number in cover photo is clearly visible to the naked eye but has been artificially enhanced for photographic purposes.

Dear Alice and Hugo   March 4, 1983

It was wondrful of you to come to speak to my classes.
You both gave something that they never could have gotten
out of a history book.
Thanks so much for sharing yourselves with these young
people. I am convinced real learning comes from human
communication - particularly when it concerns history.
What I find hard to believe is that the second World
War is history for so many generationswhen it is part
of our lifetime.
    You were both remarkable and my students as well as
myself appreciated your willingness to talk about your
harsh, inhuman experience.
    You are also both testimony to the strength and
endurance of the human spirit because you are as beautiful
on the outside as you are on the inside....

                              Sincerely
                              Nancy Martin
                    UCSD English Dept.

The Kern Family, taken at the youngest daughter's wedding.

Dear Mrs. Kern,
    Thankyou for coming today and sharing your experiences with us. The holocaust seems so long ago but having people talk about it to us makes it seem much more real. Thankyou again,

                    Sincerly,

Dear Alice Kern,
    Thank you for taking the time to come to our class and share some of your experiences and emotions with us. Your information has helped to better inform me of what the holocaust was really like. You described this area of time better than any book I've read.
    Once again thank you for having the courage to open up and share part of your life and history.

                    Thank You,
                    Melissa Elaine Flory

Dear Mrs. Kern,

Thank You very much for coming to our class. I thought it was very interesting. I enjoyed your talking and it helped me understand alot more about everything you talked about.

Heres a poem just for you.

Mrs. Kern; I
Really like you, you're
Smiles last long whiles, you're

Kind about
Everything, no kidding, you're
Really
Nice!

Thanks Again

Love
Amy Appleby